NO
MORE
FROGS
TO KISS

NO MORE FROGS TO KISS

99 WAYS TO GIVE ECONOMIC POWER TO GIRLS

Conceived by Members of
An Income of Her Own

By Joline Godfrey

HarperBusiness
A Division of HarperCollinsPublishers

HarperCollins books may be purchased for educational, business, or sales promotional use. For information please write: Special Markets Department, HarperCollins Publishers, Inc., 10 East 53rd Street, New York, NY 10022.

FIRST EDITION

Designed by Nancy Singer
Illustrated by Mari Estrella

Library of Congress Cataloging-in-Publication Data
No more frogs to kiss : 99 ways to give economic power to girls /
    conceived by members of An Income of Her Own ; by Joline
    Godfrey. — 1st ed.
        p.   cm.
    ISBN 0-88730-659-4
    1. Vocational guidance for women. 2. Professional social-
ization. 3. Career Development. 4. Young women—Finance,
Personal. 5. Young women—Economic conditions. 6. Work—
Psychological aspects. 7. Women in business—Case studies.
I. Godfrey, Joline. II. An Income of Her Own (Organization)
HF5382.6.N6   1995
650.1'082—dc20   95-9266

---

95 96 97 98 99 ❖/RRD 10 9 8 7 6 5 4 3 2 1

For Jane

"I like making a business *hum*," she would say.
She meant that she loved the process of making all the
pieces of the business come together in a coherent and
profitable fashion. For Jane, making a business was
as artful as writing a novel, as aesthetically challenging as
making a perfect photograph, and required the same patience
and care as the tending of her beloved garden.

It was my enormous privilege to have shared adventure
and dreams with her. This book is dedicated to my
business partner, my friend, my sister, and now my spirit,
Jane Lytle

CONTENTS

FOREWORD

When I was growing up, the phrase I most often heard about work was "something to fall back on." In the terrible event that my husband-to-be died, left, or wasn't a good provider, I should have the skills to type, teach, or otherwise survive in an acceptably female occupation. It was well-intentioned advice, but its underlying message never would have been given to boys: that getting paid was a social defeat, and economic independence a punishment.

It took me years to learn what the boys around me seemed to know in their bones, as well as to learn with every paper route and summer job: that $50 earned through one's own efforts was more rewarding than $500 received as a dependent, that working in the world outside the home was a way to find an identity in the world as well as to survive, and that doing a good job could be a joy in itself.

It took me even longer to discover that the idea of an income of one's own as just "something to fall back on"—which may be a more rare phrase now, but is still one directed only at girls—was a myth even when I was hearing it. Only when I was in my thirties and feminism had begun to challenge such myths did I realize that my own mother had loved her work and the independence it gave her. After earning egg money on a family farm as a little girl, doing bookkeeping and needlework as a student, and becoming a math teacher to please her mother (for whom teaching was the ultimate thing "to fall back on"), she finally found the career of her heart as a pioneer in the "masculine" profession of newspaper journalism. Giving up her work as a reporter to follow her husband and raise my sister was the beginning of the many sacrifices of self that broke my mother's spirit, even before I was born, and turned her into the sad woman I knew. She, too, had been made to feel abnormal compared to the "feminine" myth of subservience, and a little embarrassed by her working-class mother, who was always economically active, whether it was digging a kitchen garden, ghost writing sermons for the church next door, gambling on horse races, or saving money to buy a second small house as rental property. Though my mother greatly loved and admired her mother-in-law, a pioneer in vocational education, suffrage, and elected office, she also absorbed the idea that this upper-middle-class woman's work was more acceptable because it was done under the ladylike disguise of volunteerism.

That's the amazing thing about myths. They are so powerful that we internalize them even when they contradict our deepest experience. So we blame ourselves for not conforming to their impossible standard, whether it's "happily ever after" (a marzipan coating on reality even when people only lived to be fifty), or the idea that an adult woman should be happy living in childlike dependency (even though an adult man could not).

But then, this is what myths are for: to safeguard the status quo by getting us to mistrust what we see through our own eyes—to deflect anger onto self-blame.

Think about it: women in poor communities earn money and become strong because they don't expect to find husbands who earn enough for two, yet they are made to feel ashamed of their own strength, and even to envy the dependent woman "above" them. Women who love their work are punished for being selfish or "like men" and rewarded only if they pretend to work to pay for family "extras." As for homemakers—who work harder, longer hours, and for less pay than any other class of worker in the nation—they are called "women who don't work," have far less economic security than, say, their husband's business partner would have, and find themselves either wrongly disparaged or wrongly resented for "not working."

There must be a better way—and there is.

No single book can dispel all the myths much less outline a better way in all its diversity, but the one in your hands takes on this task early, radically, and with spirit.

For one thing, its pages are full of examples—real-life, imaginative, multicultural examples—of girls who are succeeding at enterprises that many would still think unlikely for adult women. Girls themselves will be inspired by these stories. After all, unless you've seen a deer, it's hard to see a deer. That's why nothing is more valuable than role models. As a byproduct, however, I wouldn't be surprised if adult women pick up this book for its value to the next generation and also find themselves moved to action by the realization "If a girl can do this, so can I!"

For another thing, this book shows adults how to help girls discover the self-respect that comes only from developing their own talents and finding their own independence—and to do it *before* the confusing fog of "happily ever after" descends. As Carol Gilligan argues in her own revolutionary research on girls' loss of voice and self-confidence in adolescence, our most important task is to strengthen healthy rebellion in young girls. Though they may still have to go underground for a while in this very gender-bound society, they will know that their authentic self is okay, strong, not at fault. Later, if they decide to take a life companion, they will be more likely to create an equal partnership, not an unequal dependency. If they decide to give birth, they will be better equipped to raise a child, without paying the patriarchal price of motherhood: giving birth to someone else instead of oneself.

This book also takes a giant step beyond salaried work. Because it is written with the understanding that race and sex are still used to create cheap labor pools—that most women working outside the home are in pink-collar, mostly female job ghettos—its pages are filled with examples of women and girls of all races who have started their own businesses. Instead of learning to please a boss, they are working to please themselves. Instead of conforming so they won't get fired, they are innovating so they can supply a unique service or product. Not only is this entrepreneurial route one all immigrant groups have found crucial—in the paid work force, women are an immigrant group, too—but its freedom may be as important as its degree of profit. After all, if we are ever to have a women's movement that is as strong as its convictions, some of us must have jobs we can't be fired from.

In addition to the ideas for change that are *in* this book, others will flow *from* it. Not only will business and financial independence change girls, for instance, but they are likely to change business and paid work. With the self-confidence to combine the world of paid work with the cultural expectations rooted in families, these energetic new women will pioneer flexible work patterns that will allow both women and men to be nurturing parents. They also bring with them into the workplace some of the values of work in the home—which, however unpaid, is highly personal, the opposite of the "alienated labor" assumed by male economists and male workers whose only experience is a fragmented, impersonal task.

As the only group too large and too vital to the human maintenance done in families to be integrated into the economic structure as it exists, females of all races are the one group that must transform every part of the workforce. For starters, we can never be equal outside the home until men are equal inside it. Until men are raising children and doing family tasks as much as women are, women will continue to be on strike, consciously or otherwise, against the simple impossibility of doing two full-time jobs; a strike that already consists of everything from turning meal production and child care into professions that pay for the first time, to a U.S. rate of population growth that has plunged below replacement level.

If men want us to have babies—whether individually as one father or collectively in businesses and governments—they must either take away our reproductive freedom and turn our bodies back into private property (as some are trying to do), or recognize the value and reward of raising the next generation by doing it themselves.

The answer is blowing in the wind. Clearly, developing all of our human qualities is the goal for both women and men. Perhaps the counterpart of Take Our Daughters to Work Day, the annual creation of the Ms. Foundation for Women that focuses workplace attention on girls, should be a Take Our Sons Home Day, emphasizing that as "women can do what men can do," "men can do what women can do."

If girls are raised to be as active outside the home as boys and boys are raised to be equally active inside it, there will not only be no more frogs to kiss—but no more frogs.

Gloria Steinem

ACKNOWLEDGMENTS

In 1994 the annual retreat for adult members of An Income of Her Own was held at the Westerbeke Ranch in California. Women from all over the country came together to discuss ways to give economic power to the next generation. Their ideas are captured in this book, and their names are listed below. After that, other women offered up suggestions for improving the economic well-being of girls. We are deeply grateful for their energy, vision, and imagination (not to mention their sense of humor and adventure). They are all women who kiss no frogs!

Denise Bredfeldt
Gillian Brown
Rita Burgett
Dori Cismowski
Martha Deevy
Barbara Dowd
Deborah Gale
Sara Hughes
Emily Hull-Parsons
Lela Jahn
Lynn Karlson

Jane Lytle
Julie McCue
Judith Musick
Ruth Owades
Kirby Sack
Dana Serleth
Vivian Shimoyama
Olga Enciso Smith
Anne Tuohy
Amy Umland
Solange Van Der Moer

And for the help and support that helped realize this book, gratitude and tribute must be paid to four people: Lynn Karlson, an indispensable part of the AIOHO team, and the person whose faxes, competence, and good judgment I rely on regularly; my friend and colleague

Georgeann Manville, without whose constant aid, good humor, and encouragement the book would not have been possible; Jolee Reed, a tenacious and persistent researcher; and Jeff Gill—humanist, friend, and spirit, the one who reminds me regularly that there is "magic in the dream."

Acknowledgment and thanks must also go to the National Association of Women Business Owners, that group of pioneering women who are tireless advocates for women business owners everywhere. As mentors, scholarship providers, and role models, their support of young women is evidence of a commitment to the next generation that really *will* make a difference. Patty DeDominic, Delores Ratcliffe, Susan Bari, Carolyn Elman, Betsy Myers, and Lindsey Johnson, all leaders of organizations making a profound difference in the economic lives of women, have also made invaluable contributions to AIOHO and the thinking behind this book. And a warm thank you to Judy Cobbs of Girls Inc., and Susan Switzer, of Girls Scouts of the USA. Both women have generously shared their immense knowledge of girls with me.

INTRODUCTION

For too long, the only security available to women came in the form of myths, marriage, or romantic legends. Handsome princes, silver slippers, and talking mirrors were offered up as symbols of love and safety. If she would just let down her golden hair, spin the gold, tend the right beast, or kiss the right frog, she was told, all would turn out well. She would be rich, beautiful, and well cared for by the man of her dreams. And if spells cast by fairy godmothers didn't work—well, the father who knew best (or maybe Riley, the one who didn't) would encourage marriage to a good man who would provide for her and the kids.

Recently, as it has become painfully obvious that neither miracles nor marriage will assure the safety of girls and women, a new solution is proliferating: self-defense classes, which teach women how to shoot a gun or pummel an attacker, have become staples of informal education programs everywhere.

Less romantic perhaps, and certainly less lethal, this book offers a third solution: economic power for girls. We all want our daughters—and granddaughters, the friends of daughters, our sisters, our nieces, and all girls everywhere—to have options. If they are in a dead-end job, we want them to be able to get out. If they are in an unsafe relationship, we want them to be able to leave. If they are in any kind of jeopardy, we want them to have the economic power to make choices that provide safe passage, safe shelter, time, or the resources necessary to have choices.

No More Frogs to Kiss is intended to help us provide the next generation with the knowledge and experiences needed to assure their economic well-being. When one young college woman said to me, "It's easier to talk about sex than money!" she spoke for too many girls and women. Although we've come a long way in opening doors for young women, we've not gone far enough in teaching them about money, economic responsibility, assets, ownership, and the power that comes from having an "income of her own." Two-thirds of all minimum-wage jobs are still held by women, and 40 percent of all working women make wages below the poverty level. Across race and class, economic safety is precarious for girls and women.

Three forces now press on us to give girls the tools and the support they need to attain economic safety. *First* is the emergence of an economic environment in which the ability to "make a job" rather than expecting to "take a job," is a basic survival skill for adults and young people alike. No longer is it enough to teach kids how to write a resumé, do an interview, and network for jobs. Now we must encourage the instinct to initiate, the ability to imagine, and the economic literacy necessary for planning a sound economic future.

The emphasis on entrepreneurship that you will note in this guide is not intended to distract girls from pursuing professions and jobs they are interested in. Rather, we suggest that if she wants to be a doctor or a lawyer, you help her think in terms of "owning the practice." If she wants to be a car mechanic, suggest that she can also own the garage. And if she wants to work in a traditional company, help her develop the entrepreneurial skills and initiative that will give her the best "job security" she can find.

Second is the changing roles of women and men. As women have begun to experience themselves as economic beings—able to pursue careers, demand equal pay, and exercise the power that accompanies economic independence, men have begun to consider the options related to being something *in addition* to economic beings. No longer cast simply as "primary breadwinners" or considered "real men" only if they are economically superior, many men now see the advantages of economic equity and shared economic power. And the concomitant responsibility of adults is to make sure we provide girls with the knowledge and skills needed to make the more flexible roles of women and men really viable.

Third, and finally, the force that came to the fore in the nineties is a new awareness of the needs of girls. Thanks to the impetus of the AAUW study, *How Schools Shortchange Girls*, published in 1991 by the American Association of University Women, other researchers and journalists began to publish material that pointed out the vulnerability of girls. Judy Mann's book *The Difference*, Myra and David Sadker's *Failing at Fairness*, and groundbreaking research conducted by Carol Gilligan and her associates have caused us to focus on the developmental needs of young women. And now, having identified the *needs* of girls, we can turn our attention to the things we can *do* to raise a new generation of confident, responsible, and economically healthy young women.

This book is a joyful signal that girls need no longer be vulnerable to frogs that don't turn into princes, systems that aren't girl friendly, or forces that conspire to keep them outside the economic web of the nation. Mothers and fathers, sisters and brothers, friends, educators, community advocates, and business leaders can change the world for girls—by helping them to change the world themselves.

Go ahead, use just ONE of the ideas in this book and give a girl something other than a frog to kiss; give her the economic power to hire him if she wants!

Joline Godfrey

HOW TO USE THIS BOOK

The book is composed of three kinds of information: actions you can take to give economic power to girls; stories about women entrepreneurs; and snapshot numbers aimed at giving you a quick look at the economic realities currently facing girls and women.

Use the book as you would a good cookbook or a hiker's guide to national parks. Browse, experiment, combine, and recombine activities appropriate to the age of the girls in your life and/or the needs of your community. Pull together a group of friends to take on some activities, use others as opportunities to work one-on-one with a young woman you know.

The vignettes of entrepreneurs that accompany each of the action suggestions are offered as stories to be shared with young women of role models who exemplify the important contributions—social and economic—that women make. The women selected are a very tiny sample of the 6.5 million women business owners in the United States and the uncounted nonprofit organizations founded and run by women. They are a fraction of the energy, vision, and courage that is available for the next generation to build on. But in their stories is tangible proof that women are a critical mass, a powerful resource for the growth and development of young women.

The action suggestions described on each page, facing each role model's story, are offered as part of a full campaign in economic literacy for girls—but the lessons herein will be useful to sons, brothers, and the male children of friends as well. Try them out in the order that suits you. But be consistent. Don't let a week pass without some action related to the economic empowerment of girls.

The numbers interspersed between entrepreneurial role models and the action ideas may make you righteously angry. They serve as reminders of why the task of giving girls economic power is so vital.

Refer to the book frequently. When it becomes dogeared and worn with use you will know that you have poured heart and energy into a healthy future for girls. Above all, have fun—at An Income of Her Own we teach kids that "business isn't spinach" and that only when you combine the passions of your life with the pursuit of financial independence are you being true to yourself. So approach this guide with a playful spirit. *No More Frogs to Kiss* is the first "antifairy tale" that truly allows a girl to live "happily ever after"!

PART 1

THINGS TO DO
WITH GIRLS

The actions suggested here can be considered ideas for mentoring, but one might also think of them as gifts to the next generation, an investment in the future. One need not be a "material girl" to care about economic well-being and the financial development of young women.

This section describes activities that you can share with one or more girls: maybe a daughter or a niece, perhaps your "Little Sister" or the child of a friend. They are experiential in nature and require a certain amount of "face time."

For people whose plates are already too full, this may seem like quite a challenge. But if as a society we have a responsibility to provide a basic safety net—decent education, safety, shelter, and justice—as individuals we also have an obligation to make sure each child growing up has access to the people, information, and experiences that will enable them to flourish. Time spent with girls now will change the very fabric of the future. Don't stint, this may be one of the best investments of time you will ever make!

Assunta Ng has described herself as a quiet, obedient child, considered among the "least likely to succeed" of her peers at school.

"I was not well liked by the teachers and I simply did not stand out," she remembers. "I was not encouraged to dream about anything. If I could get out of the house at all, I could be a teacher, nurse, or secretary; nobody ever encouraged me to do more.

Raised in Canton, China, she took the national standardized test required for Chinese high school seniors and scored in the top 100 of the 35,000 who took the exam. Stunned by her performance, she began to dream. Suffering financial barriers, parental disapproval, and few social resources, she struggled to obtain an education. Making her way to the United States, she entered college in Washington State and began to thrive.

Assunta Ng became a teacher but discovered that teaching was not the right profession for her. In 1982 she established the Chinese Seattle Post, *the first Chinese-language newspaper published in the Pacific Northwest in half a century. She says, "Because I am running my own business, every day is exciting and new. I wouldn't want to work for anyone else. I am shaping my own destiny."**

---

*Lindsey Johnson and Jackie Joyner-Kersee, *A Woman's Place Is Everywhere* (New York: MasterMedia, 1994), p. 170.

BUSINESS NEWS FOR GIRLS

Help her focus on news about business. Give her a subscription to *Equal Means* (510-549-9995) or *Turned-On Business* (800-350-2978), magazines specifically for younger women that deal with economic empowerment and social values. Clip articles about teen entrepreneurs from newspapers and magazines. *Black Enterprise* has a semiregular feature called "Kidpreneurship." Frequently *Inc., Entrepreneur,* and other business magazines will focus on kids. *Seventeen* magazine has begun a special section on careers, too, which sometimes refers to teen entrepreneurship. Keep an eye out and help her build a scrapbook about young people and their businesses. Once a month find time to discuss one of the articles with her. A young Japanese exchange student visiting Minneapolis was asked to explain her apparently avid interest in business. "I used to steal my father's *Business Week* and take it to high school with me," she explained. "I loved reading that magazine and got many ideas from it!"

Harvard Business School grad Ruth Owades worked at CML Group, Inc., a mail order house in Massachusetts. Conscientious and successful, Ruth went to her boss at CML with an idea for a mail order catalog that would appeal to the home gardener. He told her it was an idea that wouldn't work. Frustrated by his lack of imagination—and his unwillingness to trust her with an idea— Owades left CML in 1978 to found Gardener's Eden. In 1982 she sold her company to Williams Sonoma for $1 million.

Five years later, having grown the company fivefold, Ruth left Williams Sonoma and took a year off. During this time, another breakthrough business idea emerged: she would use her knowledge of direct mail to fly fresh flowers straight from growers to customers. Calyx and Corolla now sells flowers to football players and fathers, rock stars and writers, kids who give flowers for Mother's Day and lovers who mark Valentine's Day with a flair. Ruth remembers that as a young girl she was told that "girls couldn't do math." These days, Ruth works with very large numbers as she manages her multimillion-dollar, international business. For information about her mail order flowers, call 800-800-7788.

UNIT 2

TAKE OUR DAUGHTERS TO WORK*

Take somebody's daughter to work with you—both on the official day marked by the public education campaign sponsored by the Ms. Foundation for Women (fourth Thursday in April) and at another time during the year. Swap "daughters" with a friend to make sure young women see a variety of work settings and possibilities. If you are hosting a girl, try the following:

Arrange for her to interview two people in charge of products or services.

Invite her to attend a staff meeting, and ask her opinion on the agenda items.

Suggest she write a report on the visit for her school paper: what did she see, what did she like, what didn't she like?

Find someone to talk about how the company was started and why.

Find ads describing the company and ask what they tell her about it.

Show her an annual report for the company. Depending on her age and readiness, discuss the story told by the report.

Suggest she ask five people to define "bottom line" for her.

Have her collect a list of words she hears during the day that you can discuss with her later.

Ask her which jobs she can imagine herself in and why.

For more ideas, call the Ms. Foundation for Women at 800-676-7780.

*Take Our Daughters to Work was established in 1992 by the Ms. Foundation. For more information call 212-742-2300.

━ ━ ━ ━ ━ ━ ━ ━ ━ ━ ━ ━ ━ ━ ━ ━

Less than 8 percent of organizations serving girls surveyed by the Ms. Foundation for Women serve girls 9–15, the critical years in adolescent development.*

*Nari Rhee, "Taking Our Daughters Toward a Better Future," Equal Means, 2(2), Spring 1994, p. 5.

UNIT 3

GIVE ME FIVE AND BUILD SELF-ESTEEM

Self-esteem is a major element of economic empowerment. Give teen women opportunities to focus on who they are, what's important to them, and what they're good at. One way to do that is a simple game you can play at dinner or in the car called "Give Me Five." At least once a month ask her to give you:

5 adjectives to describe herself

5 skills she could barter

5 things she does well

5 things she's read outside of school

5 times she used math that day

5 people she would like to know (and what she'll do to make that happen)

5 interesting people she's met

5 business women she's heard about or met

5 businesses she's used

5 favorite ways to spend money

5 pet peeves as a consumer

5 values she thinks are important

5 things she wants to be doing in 5 years

5 places she wants to visit 5 years from now

5 skills she has and the dollar value of each

5 accomplishments in the last week

5 things she would change in her school, community, the country, the world (how can she make $$ at this?)

Jan Davidson is the president and founder of Davidson Associates, Inc., and a pioneer in educational software. After a dozen years of teaching, she started a nonprofit tutorial center in a suburb of Los Angeles, California, bought an Apple II for $3,000, and wrote programs to drill students in vocabulary and math. These product were so well received that in 1982, Davidson formed a company to publish Math Blaster, Speed Racer, and Word Attack.

Beginning in the 1990s, the demand for educational and entertainment software increased dramatically, and Davidson experienced significant growth. Today the company has annual sales of close to $90 million and is a leader in developing, publishing, and distributing over 50 award-winning, multimedia software titles.

The company continues to focus on interactive multimedia software to meet the changing needs of users in both homes and schools. In the home market, Davidson offers many new titles for users from ages three to adult; each includes engaging graphics, lots of sound effects, animation, and solid educational content. In the school market, a new product in 1995 is Vital Links, which teachers use to help limited-English-proficient students learn about U.S. history. Roughly 40 percent of students entering school in California do not have English as their first language; thus, Davidson's attention to the needs of those individuals will make a big difference in their experiences at school and in life.

TAKE HER FOR A RIDE ON THE INFORMATION SUPERHIGHWAY

Subscribe to an on-line service or help her get on the Internet. Drawing young women onto the "information superhighway" is an important way to help them participate fully in the world of technology and information. Women's Wire, the on-line service for women (800-210-9999); E-World (800-775-4556), which includes AIOHO and the Adventures of Marisela, intrepid teen entrepreneur; Pipeline (212-267-3636); and America Online (800-827-6364) are just a few of the many services that provide access to diverse sources of information, and they are another way for girls and women to keep up to date on issues. Communicate with her regularly using e-mail, teach her how to use the "superhighway" to do research for school or for her application to AIOHO's National Business Plan Competition. Girls who grow up comfortable with computers and the information they provide access to will have greater economic options in terms of careers and professions.

THE INDIAN GIVER

Let there be no purpose in giving
  save reciprocity.
For to a people whose spirituality
  lies within Life's wholeness
Who share the gifts of the sky
and the mountains and the seas
  and the forests
Who exchange abundance
  in the circle of animal brethren
Giving is not a matter of pure
altruism and benevolence
but a mutual responsibility
To make the world
a better place.

(Source: Rebecca Adamson,
"The President's Message"
10-Year Report, 1991,
First Nations Development
Institute)

GIVING BACK

Ask her to list all the causes and issues she cares about (wolves to whales, homelessness and hunger, children's theater or Special Olympics).

Encourage her to select the cause she is interested in and discuss how she might raise money to further her cause. Suggest this be a regular part of her budget.

Explore what she might do instead of, or in addition to, giving money. Discuss the idea of social investments. Suggest she look at the differences between charity, philanthropy, and socially responsible giving.

Give her a copy of *Ben & Jerry's: The Inside Scoop*, by Fred "Chico" Lager, to learn more about a contemporary company's search for ways to balance social responsibility with fiscal responsibility. Or, if she's too young for this, take her to the Ben & Jerry's Homemade, Inc., headquarters in Waterbury, Vermont, for a tour of the factory and a slide show that tells the story in a slightly different way.

Suggest she learn something about Working Assets, the telephone company that combines the provision of long-distance service with the ability to contribute to a variety of social causes. Explore with her the reasons someone might choose Working Assets as their telephone company over one of the more traditional long-distance providers. Suggest she write to the company to learn more about how they manage concern for social causes with the need to be competitive (800-788-0898).

Nearly 75 percent of tomorrow's jobs will require the use of computers, but fewer than 33 percent of participants in computer courses and computer-related activities are girls.*

*Nari Rhee, "Taking Our Daughters Toward a Better Future," *Equal Means*, 2(2), Spring 1994, p. 7.

UNIT 6

- - - - - - - - - - - - - - - - -

LEVERAGE YOUR COMPUTER!

Share your computer (at home, at work, or find a friend who will share hers) with a girl. Take her to a software store and help her select a game or an application that interests her. Teach her to use the computer for keeping a journal, doing homework, keeping track of a hobby, creating a budget, communicating with other teens. Set aside a time that's regularly hers—hire her to do "computer chores" for you.

When sharing becomes counterproductive, work with her to develop a plan to buy one of her own (can she think of a way to earn $25/month for two years if you help with a down payment?). Or maybe you can find a used computer to get her started. Canvas local companies to find out what they do with old computers—can you create a community pool of used computers for kids?

Foghorn Press owner Vicki Morgan explains, "What we do is publish books, but it's our Books Building Community program that makes the company work." Morgan matches every new title with a nonprofit organization related to the book's subject area. The nonprofit then receives 2 to 10 percent of the proceeds of the book.

Vicki believes that investing in one's community is an important element of investing in one's business. As she puts it, "Some companies think they'll wait until they are successful, then they'll give back. But I think you have to give first, then you get back." Now publishing 17 to 25 titles a year on subjects ranging from sports to outdoor guides about camping, hiking, fishing, and even bungie jumping, Foghorn Press is growing at a rate of over 30 percent a year, making it apparent that Vicki's concept of "social entrepreneurship" is good for the bottom line.

UNIT 7

- - - - - - - - - - - - - - -

PROVIDE START-UP CAPITAL

If she needs a piece of equipment or some working capital to start a money-making project (instead of taking that part-time job as a waitress), set it up as a loan and teach her the meaning of the phrase "start-up capital." Work out a repayment plan that will keep her excited and motivated to keep the business growing. Consider requiring one-third to one-half of the gross profits from each transaction until the loan is paid back.

If the enthusiasm of the start-up period fades and the hard work of running a business is becoming increasingly clear, help her visualize goals that will keep her motivated: paying for all or part of a major purchase (school, a bike, a car—if she's older, travel, etc.) or making a contribution to a favorite cause. Alternatively, it may help to fantasize about her adult life and how the skills she's developing in her business will help her create options for her future.

Pleasant Rowland was dissatisfied with the dolls available to little girls and with the lack of knowledge about women's history that girls acquire while growing up. Putting her dissatisfaction to work, Rowland created the Pleasant Company, and introduced the American Girls Collection. Books and dolls are designed to introduce different periods in American history. The collection includes Addy, a little girl of the Civil War period, the daughter of slaves; Felicity, a colonial girl; Kirsten, a pioneer girl; Samantha, a Victorian girl; and Molly, a girl from the World War II era.

The American Girls may never replace Barbie—who seems to have a special hold, whether we like it or not— but Rowland has enlarged the vision and the knowledge of young girls all over the country with her imaginative delivery of women's history. And she runs an enormously successful business, based in Wisconsin, that she started with an advance from a book sale. For more about the American Girls Collection call 800-845-0005.

UNIT 8

HONOR WOMEN'S ECONOMIC HISTORY

Choose a day—any day that has meaning to the two of you—and turn it into an annual celebration of women's economic history.

Throw a Rosie the Riveter party and invite girls to come dressed in a costume that demonstrates how they will support themselves. Give them time to guess what each costume signifies; give prizes for the most original costume, run a game of charades based on the lives of women in history. Use Susan B. Anthony dollar coins for prizes. Provide a storyteller who can relate something about the lives of women who have opened economic doors for girls. Organize a talking circle so girls can discuss their idea of what economic independence is. Provide books and magazines and ask the girls to create a book that tells something about women's economic history. Or give them each a topic or person with their invitation and ask them to come prepared to tell a story about Madame C. J. Walker, the women textile workers in Lawrence, Massachusetts, Rosie the Riveter, women who were "firsts" in their chosen field, or other people or subjects that relate to women's economic history.

Make this an annual event!

Women comprise only 11 percent of today's technical work force.*

*Nari Rhee, "Taking Our Daughters Toward a Better Future," *Equal Means*, 2(2), Spring 1994, p. 7.

UNIT 9

COMMUNICATE COMPETENCE

When a young woman asks, "What should I do?" ask her right back, "What do you *think* you should do?"

This is one way of letting her know you think she is competent and able to think for herself. Economic power is a form of independence and must be nurtured in attitude as well as in action.

Old habits of "taking care of" girls, however well intended, often have the reverse effect of undermining their sense of possibility and mastery. Learning to be economically self-aware is, in part, a process of discovery and exploration best done with supportive mentoring and caring challenges from the adults in a young person's life.

In the mid-eighties, when Sherrie Maurer of Sharon, Vermont, started Jasmine & Bread, Inc., she had no money to pay for the necessities of starting a business: legal support, accounting, and advertising. The Small Business Administration (less supportive then than it is now for women entrepreneurs) turned down her request for a loan. And although she did get a small loan from a local bank (thanks to a lending officer willing to take a chance on her), it wasn't enough to cover all the expenses of starting a business.

But Sherrie's product, a unique catsup (now just one of a number of specialty condiments she produces), was good enough to be bartered for services. Jonathan Brownell, a lawyer who specialized in start-ups, exchanged a continuous supply of Beyond Catsup for making sure her legal basics were in order. Other friends helped her build a customer base through direct response advertising. They, too, get a never-ending supply of Sherrie's gourmet condiments. (To try Beyond Catsup, Sweet Lightning Horseradish Jelly, Bourbon Blast & Maple Glaze, or any of her other products call 802-763-7115.)

Sherrie isn't the first entrepreneur to trade goods for business help. When Ben Cohen and Jerry Greenfield were trying to get their first scoop shop ready for business they struck a deal with a friend who worked for a local contractor: Darrell Mullis became the charter member of the Ice Cream for Life Club in exchange for helping to turn a former gas station into an ice-cream shop!*

*Fred Lager, *Ben & Jerry's: The Inside Scoop* (New York: Crown Publishing, 1994), pp.19–20.

UNIT 10

INTRODUCE BARTER

Introduce a teen woman to the concept of barter. Identify assets you each have (algebra knowledge, transportation, a computer, tennis skills). Invite your friends to start a Women's Barter Network that includes teens. Suggest things she can barter. For example:

Trade an hour of errands for you for an evening's use of a scarf or a piece of jewelry.

Trade a car washing for an hour of special help with a school project.

Trade baby-sitting time for driving her around to places she wants to go.

Trade her ability to address envelopes in calligraphy for your ability to braid her hair in corn rows.

The goal is to demonstrate that even when you do not have cash, you have things of value with which you can negotiate. Care should be taken to stress that sometimes you do things for other people with no expectation of "getting something back." Historically, women have given away their skills and time without placing a value on them. This is a way to teach the difference between giving for its own sake and barter as a means of economic exchange.

Stacy Kabat is a social entrepreneur who helped focus attention on violence against women as a human rights issue. The winner of the 1994 Reebok Human Rights Award, she is the force behind Battering Women Fighting Back!, Inc. (BWFB!), a nonprofit organization devoted to educating women about domestic violence and advocating for them.

The film she co-produced, Defending Our Lives, *received an Oscar at the 1994 Academy Awards. The documentary told the story of women incarcerated for having struck back at the abusive people in their lives. Ms. Kabat maintains that "it's the combined power of education, awareness, and economic empowerment that can save women's lives." For more information on BWFB! and the film* Defending Our Lives, *call 617-354-3677.*

CREATE AN ANNUAL REPORT

Budgets get a bum rap. Maybe because so few women have felt in control of their money—or because money to budget has been scarce—budgets conjure up feelings of deprivation, or imposed authority, or inadequacy. So suggest creating a budget in the form of an annual report—yes, like the ones that companies issue. Take a trip to the library to look over annual reports together.

Some reports are dry and boring to read; others, like that of Marvel Comics, are entertaining and exciting—and they all tell stories about a company's vision.

By asking girls to write stories describing their vision for themselves, and telling the stories, partly in financial terms, you help them attach methods and plans to dreams. The table of contents for her annual report might look like this:

Mission (what I plan to accomplish this year)
Expected income (and where I think it's coming from)
Expenses (what I have to spend each month and want to spend it on)

Help her create a monthly operating budget, a cash flow statement, and a summary for her annual report.

In the year 2000, only 14 percent of jobs will be available to workers with less than a high school education—but 58 percent of women will only have a high school diploma or less.*

*Nari Rhee, "Taking Our Daughters Toward a Better Future," *Equal Means*, 2(2), Spring 1994, p. 7

UNIT 12

------ - - - - - - - - - - - -

SHOP TILL YOU DROP!

Take a teen on three shopping expeditions: 1) for food; 2) for jeans or a pair of shoes; 3) for a piece of technical equipment—a CD player, a tape recorder, or a piece of computer equipment. The goal of these expeditions is to introduce comparison shopping. (Make it clear this is a *simulation*—not the real thing!)

Before leaving for the mall or Main Street, spend some time with her looking through newspaper ads or catalogs. Have her make a list of what she wants and how much she expects to spend. Select three stores in which to get prices for each product. Ask her to explain why she thinks prices might be the same or different. Discuss trade-offs (time versus price; convenience and service versus price, etc.). Make sure she asks a store employee about product benefits and differences as she compares products.

NOTE: As with many of the suggestions in this book, sometimes a parent is not the best mentor for one's own kids. Occasionally it helps to "swap kids." You might take a neighbor's daughter on these expeditions and the neighbor might take yours!

Katy Meyer of Massachusetts entered AIOHO's 1993 National Business Plan Competition when she was just fourteen. She had recently completed an art course in which she had worked with paints on fabric. Soon after, she noticed an ad for the Competition in Sassy magazine and sent for an application. As Katy explained later, "I saw how I could combine my art with a way to make money."

Katy's entry described a plan to paint and sell silk scarves, clothing accessories, and canvas rugs. By the time of the awards ceremony, she had already put her plan into action and turned up at the ceremony, exquisite scarves in hand, ready to sell.

And sell she does; her scarves range in price from $80 to $400. Solange Van Der Moer, an advisor to the National Business Plan Competition winners and a San Francisco software entrepreneur, has been instrumental in getting Katy on the "information superhighway." Using the Internet, Katy now buys silk from countries all over the world—getting the best price and meeting people across cultures she would not otherwise have had access to. And she uses e-mail to stay in touch with Solange—3,000 miles away—for ongoing advice and business counselling.

UNIT 13

EDIT MONEY MESSAGES

Money doesn't grow on trees! What do you think I'm made of, money? Money is the root of all evil.

Sound familiar? You can probably add a few of your own versions of "money wisdom" that your parents passed on to you. Next time she says she "must have" the shoes, the dress, the new CD, take a deep breath and try a new script. Here's a sample:

Old script:

Teen: I need a new pair of running shoes.
Adult: What do you think I'm made of, money?
Teen, (*in a huff*)**:** Oh, Maaaaaaah!!!! (*Stomps off*)

New script:

Teen: I need a new pair of running shoes.
Adult: What do you plan to do to get them?

The old script is likely to lead to a battle of control (not to mention all that whining!), whereas the new script may lead to joint problem solving. In any event, with the new script, you avoid an ancient battle between kids and adults AND you present a model for real world economics, a far more important lesson than tired truisms about money.

Olga Enciso Smith was born in Peru and left that country in 1962 to attend nursing school in Detroit, Michigan. On a trip to an Indian reservation in southern California in 1965, Olga was struck by the fact that much of the Native American art had been lost. Although she continued her college education, she decided against nursing as a career and began to explore ways to keep native folk art and crafts alive and vibrant among native people.

In 1974 Olga established Machu Picchu, in northern California. Twenty years later her company has grown to be part retail store, part museum, and part educational institution. Machu Picchu started as a means of showcasing and selling the work of Peruvian artists. But today, Olga's company also features artists from Ecuador, Bolivia, Mexico, and other countries of Central and South America, as well as Native American arts and crafts. The small museum attached to her store in downtown San Jose provides a way of keeping the community educated about art created by people of many backgrounds.

Once a year Olga also leads tours to Peru to study folk art in that country. Her quarterly newsletter functions as both a mail order catalog and a journal of folk arts and crafts. Olga is spending her life pursuing the integration of art and business and finding ways to enrich our lives as well as her own. To learn more about her tours, the Machu Picchu newsletter, and her store, you can call Olga at 408-280-1860.

UNIT 14

TEACH DEFENSIVE ECONOMICS

"**W**hat you don't know can't hurt you." When it comes to money, that old saw just ain't so. Though most auto mechanics, plumbers, electricians, and other "fixers" in our lives are decent, honorable practitioners of their crafts, many still prey on the ignorance of their customers.

Traditionally, car and house repair have been "male duties" taken care of by fathers, husbands, and boyfriends. In preparation for the next century, give a teen woman some defensive intelligence: for the holidays or on her birthday, make one of her gifts a certificate for a tutoring session on basic car care, or bathroom and kitchen repairs. And next time she needs her bike fixed or a doll repaired, encourage her to fix it herself.

━ ━ ━ ━ ━ ━ ━ ━ ━ ━ ━ ━ ━ ━ ━ ━

More people in the United States work for women who own businesses than for the Fortune 500 worldwide!*

*National Foundation for Women Business Owners, "The New Economic Work Force," Data Report (Washington, D.C.), 1992, p. 3.

UNIT 15

SEE THE GRATEFUL DEAD

The gross sales of the Grateful Dead in 1993 was $50 million. Take a teen to a rock concert and use it as a business case study. (Don't forget to enjoy the music!) See if she can name all the ways they make money: ticket sales, recording royalties, television specials, licensing agreements for T-shirts, coffee mugs, stadium blankets, etc. Then have her identify how other companies make money on a concert: equipment rental, providing security, technical support, limo rentals, etc.

The point of this music economics lesson is to demonstrate the ways one can combine a passion with business, as well as showing the interdependency of businesses. And with job security fading as quickly as moonbeams in the dawning sun, it won't hurt to point out the advantages of learning how to make jobs rather than "taking jobs."

Fran Sussner Rodgers describes herself as a child of the six-ties, daughter of Polish immigrants, a woman who never liked working for someone else. As the founder of Work/Family Directions she has helped revolutionize the corporate world's attitudes about work/family policy and company behavior. Her 1989 article in the Harvard Business Review, *"Business and the Facts of Family Life," marked a turning point in that publication's willingness to take the subject seriously.*

Work/Family Directions educates managers about the realities of changing family imperatives: households with single parents or working couples who cannot support the systems that were once so functional to corporate America. And as the over three hundred Work/Family employees educate, they also help companies revamp policies, change operating practices, and generally ease the transition from one century to the next. Work/Family Directions can be reached in Boston at 800-248-3312.

UNIT 16

ENCOURAGE HER TO QUESTION AUTHORITY!

Some days it seems that young people question everything, so why should you encourage her to question authority? Because, for some reason, even girls who seem the most contrary grow up reluctant to question "experts."

So she doesn't get a second opinion about the operation her regular doctor recommends. The word of her insurance agent may be enough to buy that new policy. And the lawyer she talks to about a contract may reassure her enough that she signs it without reading the fine points.

Trust is a good thing for young women to develop. Blind, unquestioning trust can be very expensive. Take her with you when you get a second opinion. Do it even if it doesn't feel comfortable—remember, you're a role model now!

Marsha Seidman left IBM in 1977 and started Crwth, her first software company, with a loan of $30,000 from family members. She nurtured the company with hard work and attention to detail—there were no magic beans or fairy godmothers. And when the opportunity to sell for several million dollars to Robert Maxwell presented itself in 1989, she took it.

Then she took time out and moved to a beach house in Malibu. But her entrepreneurial brain would not nap. Walking the beach, watching the waves, she tried to unravel the previous years, to understand the factors that had led to the growth and sale of her company. Analytical, careful, organized, she realized that it was the systems she had created to manage her company that had made a difference.

LaunchPac, a software product, was born as Marsha beach-combed the Pacific shore. Seidman spent the next year with Pam Dong, a former Crwth colleague developing the product. And then it was time to find out how the market would react to it. At about the same time she began to meet other women who owned companies—they heard about her product and asked to see it. They wanted help launching and running their companies; they were eager to learn and receptive to her product. Today, her marketing plan is directed almost entirely to women business owners: "Women recognize that they don't know it all," she says. "They're learners and open to tools and products that will help them grow and improve." For information on LaunchPac, contact Marsha at P.O. Box 2489, Malibu, CA 90265.

ADMIRE THE LOTUS

The software, not the position! You don't know what a spreadsheet is? You haven't worked on Excel yourself? Quicken is still a way to describe your pulse when you have to face a large audience?

Economic literacy and computer skills are not genetic gifts. What you may not know, your student or daughter can learn. Or maybe you have a niece, the daughter of a friend, or a Little Sister who can recognize a baking tin but is not yet able to whip up a balance sheet.

Get her a lesson. Girls and teen women do not need the financial acumen of a CPA, but familiarity with how to create a cash flow statement and a balance sheet will make them more comfortable later with controlling their own financial reality. If you can't teach her, ask a friend to spend time with her. See if there's a class at the local Y that might provide an introduction to money and the computer.

*Currently, forty percent of young women—regardless of class or race—become pregnant at least once before the age of twenty.**

*Nari Rhee, "Taking Our Daughters Toward a Better Future," *Equal Means*, *2*(2), Spring 1994, p. 8.

UNIT 18

SAVE MONEY: NEGOTIATE!

When—and how—did you learn that some things in life are negotiable? After you paid more for that first car than you wanted to? When you signed a contract that ended up costing more than you'd bargained for?

Some girls tell us that talking about money "is more personal than sex." To avoid the discomfort that comes with such an attitude, girls may try to get a financial transaction over with as quickly as possible—undermining their negotiating strength in the bargain.

The next time someone you know is going to buy a new car, ask them to take along a teen woman and let her observe the negotiation process. Make sure she understands what she's listening for and what the goal is. Or take her to a flea market and help her negotiate a price for something that catches her eye.

Whether negotiating contracts at work or in one's personal life, it's easier if a girl is taught at a young age that this is part of the normal process of coming to an agreement on an exchange—for a car, a house, or services—and that negotiating can be a slow, messy, yet artful process. Girls who are taught to view the process as one of reciprocity and good judgment will grow up better able to act in their own best interest.

Although born in El Salvador, Marti McMahon grew up near the Great Lakes, where she learned that there were three things she really liked to do: cruise, entertain, and make gourmet meals. In the mid-seventies she moved to San Francisco and put those three loves together in a business—Pacific Marine Yachts Charter and Dining Cruises.

She refurbished her first boat herself—a 49-passenger vessel—in the yard behind her house. The Pacific Adventurer, *as it was christened, was the first of an entire fleet that now plies the waters of San Francisco Bay. Her most recent addition was too large to build in her backyard—the luxurious, 700-passenger* San Francisco Spirit.

Her instincts and experience, and an unerring awareness of her clients' needs, have helped her business grow over the years. Marti's clients include royalty and reporters, conventioneers and corporate execs, senators and singers. Security frogmen have inspected the undersides of her boats to make sure her clients are safe, and paparazzi frequent her ships waiting for the picture that will make the cover of People *or* Parade. *The first celebration of teen winners for the National Business Plan Competition was held on board one of her ships. To find out how to cruise with Marti, call 800-2-YACHTS.*

UNIT 19

ENCOURAGE HER TO DO WHAT SHE LOVES

In 1987 Marsha Sinetar wrote *Do What You Love and the Money Will Follow*; then in 1992 Nanette Hucknell published *Finding Your Work, Loving Your Life*. There are now many books, classes, and videotapes with the same message: people who integrate the pursuit of work with attention to what matters most to them enjoy the most satisfying work.

Previous generations have been encouraged to seek *sensible, safe* careers. But now, a "safe career" is a vanishing animal and "sensible" is in the eyes of the beholder. Better to help a girl identify the interests and issues that really matter to her and help her build work around those things, rather than away from what she loves. Help her pay attention to the most essential elements of who she is—therein will lie the path to economic well-being in a field she is committed to. Terrie Lonier, the author of *Working Solo*, calls it following your "passion center" while pursuing your profit centers.

The Mills Sisters—not the singing team—own five Body Shop franchises in the Washington, D.C., area. They established the first American franchise of the U.K.-based company. Helen Jr. (yes, named after Mom—Helen Sr.), Maryann, and a friend, Susan Spriggs, established Soapbox Trading to make money and a contribution to their community. They have done both. One of their most successful shops is in Georgetown, a thriving shop whose daily traffic on some days rivals that of Grand Central Station.

Since running five retail shops apparently isn't enough to soak up all their energy, the three take on other ventures as well. Among the latest: founding a T-shirt manufacturing company staffed entirely by people who are homeless, jobless, or in rehabilitation. And Helen Jr. is the co-founder of Businesses for Social Responsibility, an education and advocacy organization pressing for ethical management in business. These are women for whom multitasking is second nature. And, they report, "Our books balanced within a few dollars last year."

MAKE HER A ROLODEX GIRL

President Clinton's Rolodex is now legendary: from the time he was a young boy he was keeping track of everyone he met. If your entrepreneur-to-be doesn't have one already, give her an address book and talk with her about the importance of keeping track of people she meets, what they do, what they are interested in. Give her a few good numbers to start with—do you have a friend in a field she has expressed interest in? Give her the contact and suggest she call your friend and invite her for coffee or tea—just to talk.

If she's shy, offer to go with her. Make sure you discuss the difference between building reciprocal relationships and simply using people, but teach her the value of creating a web of support that will last a lifetime.

Nine percent of women-owned businesses (about the same as all businesses) have annual sales over $1 million!*

*National Foundation for Women Business Owners, "The New Economic Work Force," Data Report (Washington, D.C.), 1992, p. 13.

VOTE FOR ECONOMIC POWER

Susan B. Anthony and her sisters worked hard to secure the vote for American women in 1919. And in the last decade women's contributions to EMILY's List and The WISH List have helped place record numbers of women in office. But until women vote regularly and in big numbers, we will continue to see the "feminization of poverty." Vote, take a young woman with you when you vote, make sure she votes when she comes of age, discuss the issues with her. Study the candidates and their positions on women and economic issues. Most budget cuts fall on the heads of women and children. Make sure the next generation sees the connection between voting and economic power.

As the owner of Esprit, Susie Tompkins has managed her company through demographic change, economic recession, and the usual problems of a fast-growing company. Throughout, she has remained committed to an activist agenda that insists that corporate profits can be attained in tandem with concern for environment, people, and education.

One of the most unusual and courageous campaigns we've seen was a label signed by Susie that stated, "Don't buy this if you don't need it." Her concern for environmental awareness and responsible behavior was behind this highly unorthodox message. And though some of Susie's business decisions may appear unorthodox, the company has been around since 1968, resumés arrive at the rate of a thousand a month, and the company continues to set a standard for combining fashion sense and common sense on social and environmental issues.

UNIT 22

MAKE ROLE MODELS VISIBLE

Six and a half million women own businesses in the United States. They own over a third of all businesses and employ more people than the *Fortune* 500. They have financial clout both as individuals and as a collective entity. But they are still often invisible—hiding in plain sight—a powerful, invisible, community force.

Spend a Saturday introducing girls to the invisible women in your community: the dentist who owns her own practice, the lawyer who hung out her own shingle, the owner of the local real estate office, the woman who holds a local franchise for McDonald's or The Body Shop. If you are in a large urban area, you probably have women who own large companies: maybe a mail order catalog business or an airplane leasing firm, or a large fashion design company. Make sure you also introduce her to women who work from their homes (a caterer or a calligrapher, perhaps).

It's important for girls to see women who own businesses not just as individual and interesting "novelties," but as a dynamic and powerful group, members of the community whose businesses contribute to the health of that community as well as to their own well-being.

Terrie Williams graduated from Brandeis University and the Columbia University School of Social Work. While she was working at New York Hospital in Manhattan, Miles Davis, the famous musician, was admitted to the hospital.

Curious about the jazzman, she went to his room, introduced herself, and started a friendship with him that was to last until his death in 1993. While Mr. Davis was still in the hospital, Williams decided to move into the world of public relations and make Miles Davis a client. Eventually, she made that happen. Eddie Murphy was her first client and today the Terrie Williams Agency has one of the most exciting client lists in the country.

It is the combination of Terrie's skills at building relationships, her riveting ability to focus, and her amazing energy that has caused her company to grow—without resorting to more "hospital recruitments!" as she puts it. But aside from her importance to her clients, Williams has become a serious role model to young people in the world of public relations. Garnering award after award, she received the prestigious New York Woman in Communications Matrix Award in 1992. Williams was the first African-American woman to be selected in the twenty-five-year history of the awards.

UNIT 23

HELP BUILD BIG DREAMS

In interviews with teens, we are often struck by the narrow limits of their dreams. Although there is nothing inherently better about big dreams than small dreams, we think girls ought to *choose* the scope of their dreams, rather than be limited by them. Try these dream-enhancing exercises with her—remember, the goal is not to diminish the visions she has in her head, or to communicate that bigger is better, but to expand the possibilities among which she may choose to set her life goals:

1. Next time you hear her admiring someone in the news, ask her if she would like to do what they do and help her think about what one would do to pursue that goal.

2. Even from the time you start reading her Dr. Seuss books, make sure you also read and tell stories about women who have achieved big dreams—let her know that she can do things to change the world too. (*Cinder-Elly* by Frances Minters is one of our favorite books about girls who take charge.)

3. Suggest she think about becoming the President of the United States, the head of the Sierra Club, the owner of a large chain of surf shops (we don't suggest that all dreams have to be equally noble!). Have her write a plan for what she might do to attain these goals.

Currently, women-owned businesses receive only 1.6 percent of all government contracts. At the current rate of growth, they will make the federal goal of 5 percent in 2027, just when the next generation comes of age.*

*Women's Business Exclusive, 1(8), November 1993, p. 1.

UNIT 24

"MISSTERY" OF TIME!

While we don't want to raise a generation of Mad Hatters constantly looking at their watches, muttering about being late, and guarding minutes like misers, we do think that one way for girls to grow up with a sense of control and power is to experience mastery (or *miss*tery) over their time. Try these ideas to show the connections between time and control:

1. Give a bonus for particular chores done (properly) in a certain time period—deducting money for late completion.

2. Give her an appointment book and ask her to keep track of her time so she has at least 20 percent work (homework, chores, part-time work, etc.) and 20 percent fun (sports, television, club activities, etc.) scheduled in each week. Let her be in charge of making adjustments to meet the goals.

3. Suggest she reserve special time with you each week—plan a meal, an event, or even a phone call. Respect the time set and if an appointment must be changed, make sure you consult her to reschedule, not just peremptorily giving her a new time.

Etienne LeGrand, Kathy Keeley, and Connie Evans are women who champion micro-lending and in the process help the working poor, immigrant women, and homeless women reclaim their lives. Etienne is the executive director of Women's Initiatives for Self-Employment in San Francisco, California. Kathy was the founder of Wedco, the first of the U.S. micro-lending programs for women. And Connie is the president of the Women's Self-Employment Project in Chicago.

Their programs are critical interventions in the lives of women without resources. Not only have they created organizations that provide access to loans of $50 to $25,000, but they offer resources that recognize the more complicated needs of the whole person. Offering contacts and referrals, emotional support, encouragement, and training or access to training where needed, they create safety nets that help women manage the process of becoming economically self-sufficient. But more than that, they offer a place where women can dare, learn, and become economically powerful.

As the economy—and the priorities of the nation—shifts, emphasizing employment self-sufficiency over job security, programs like those provided by Keeley, LeGrande, and Evans will be increasingly essential to people who must learn to create their own economic opportunities.

UNIT 25

OPPORTUNITY COSTS!

Helping girls come to grips with the reality that opportunities often have costs attached, is one way to help them develop judgment skills—and begin the process of valuing their choices. Rather than telling girls what they cannot do (you can't hang out with that crowd, you can't go there, you can't have that dress), help them make their own judgments based on the costs of their decisions. For example:

She: I just want to stay up a little longer.

You: Let's say you need a total of fifty-six hours of sleep every week, If you stay up later tonight, where will you make that up?

or

She: I've joined the Bikers Club. *(Teens don't always ask first—if you know at all, it might be accidentally!)*

You: What might that get in the way of?

She: There's a sale at the mall—I can get a new pair of jeans for half-price.

You: That same amount of money will cover three movies—which do you want to do?

Showing her she can make choices—even wrong ones—as long as she is aware of the costs associated with those choices is one way to help her build a sense of responsibility as well as confidence in her decision-making ability.

Jackie Farley's company arose from her own journey of reflection and finding a "centerpoint." A former corporate woman, she turned an avocation into her vocation. While managing an employee wellness operation she had founded for one of the largest manufacturing companies in the Midwest, she became interested in why people change and what stops them. To uncover answers to this question, she organized women's groups and ran retreats for executive couples.

As she became more involved with the quest for answers in other people's lives, she began to explore her own needs. Eventually she left corporate life to bring her personal life and her work into greater alignment. The result was CenterPoint, a place for women to take a deep breath and literally take time out for themselves. Located in Aspen, Colorado, Jackie's retreat is based on the principle that women gain most from sharing their solutions to complicated lives.

For information on this respite from an over-full life, call Jackie at 303-920-2393.

CO-OP CDS?

Introduce cooperative buying. If she's going to use her lunch money to buy CDs or tapes anyway, offer to help her organize a music-buying club. Are there stores in town that will guarantee a lower price to a group of ten teens who will buy exclusively from them? It's worth asking—it's especially worth having her ask!

Suggest she volunteer time at a co-op food store, if there is one in the community. This will introduce her to the methods and values of cooperative working and buying.

Lack of an economic safety net is dangerous.

Nationally, 50 percent of all homeless women and children are on the streets because of violence in the home and no financial backup.*

*Domestic Violence: The Facts (Boston: Battered Women Fighting Back!, 1994), p. 5.

UNIT 27

ECONOMIC FILM FESTIVAL

Have a "movie party" complete with popcorn, brownies, and discussion. Make it a marathon Saturday or a series of evenings over a month's time. Movie suggestions:

Baby Boom
Disclosure
9 to 5
Pat and Mike
Rosie the Riveter
Working Girl

Encourage the girls to discuss what they saw and felt about each of the movies—as well as the movies as a group. What messages did they think were being sent about work; what feelings did they get from watching the movies; which characters did they identify with; how do they imagine their own working lives? If they were to make their own movie about work, what would the story be?

Personal pain was the driving force behind Sherry Poe's growth as an entrepreneur. In 1971 she was nineteen and hitchhiking with a friend to her job as a jeweler's apprentice a few miles from her college campus. When the friend was dropped off first, the driver pulled a gun on Sherry, threatened her life, and drove her to the countryside, where she was raped. The trauma that followed led to bulimia, chronic hepatitis, and eventually welfare.

She knew she could either give in to it all and die or fight her way back to health. She got a job selling Mary Kay Cosmetics, became a sales manager at a health and fitness company, and finally was a consultant with a giftware manufacturer. Because of a back injury developed while exercising, she was inspired to design athletic shoes specifically for women. Thus the inception of Rykä. A spot on Oprah (America's wealthiest female entrepreneur, by the way) helped bring some much needed atttention to the brand.

Her success with her company made it possible for her to establish the not-for-profit Rykä Rose (Regaining One's Self Esteem) Foundation, which is committed to ending violence against women. In January 1995 Rykä entered into a merger agreement with L.A. Gear to provide much needed financing.

UNIT 28

INTRODUCE THE MALL GAME

To play the Mall Game with a group of young women you need:

1. 4 to 8 girls (playing in pairs)
2. A mall or shopping district
3. A printed form for each team, which includes:
   a. the budget
   b. the required purchase items
   c. time limit

The girls go to shops to find the items they need on the list. When they make a "purchase" they note the item with the price, and get a salesperson's initials for verification. Make sure they have time to talk with their partners about a spending/buying strategy. Don't make it a race, although the game should not go for more than a half-day. Who wins? The team that got the most for their money: they completed the required list and made "extra" purchases.

Cathryn Murray is the founder of the Global Teen Club, an international newsletter where teenagers discuss their issues and concerns. Now in college, she started the newsletter when she was 16. In 1994, at the age of 18, Cathryn's organization became an official non-profit organization in the state of California, making it possible for her to raise funds for her enterprise from foundations. Though she charges a subscription fee, she also finds ways to keep teens who can not afford to pay involved with the newsletter.

Cathryn understands what that's like. She held multiple jobs all through her high school years. Some days she starts at three or four in the morning and may not end her "day" until after midnight. Cathryn communicates an inner vision that allows her to study, work, care for her chronically ill mother, and continue to expand her own venture—with remarkably few resources or support. To sign up a teen you know for the Global Teen Club write to GTC International, 3120 Oak Road, #309, Walnut Creek, CA 94596-2076.

PUT HER ON A PAYROLL!

Talk is cheap. Make sure you put your money where your mouth is. Put a young woman on your payroll at home or at work. Value her time. Help her figure out what her time is worth! Suggest that she ask friends what the going rate is for the job you are proposing. Help her do a cost analysis of her time (make sure she includes travel, expenses, money spent to get the job, etc.). Or make sure if she gets a job mowing lawns that she's paid as much as the boys in your neighborhood!

It's tempting to use girls as cheap labor—but that's the problem. Girls and women have been cheap labor too long. As a result, they grow up not knowing, or demanding pay that reflects their real worth. Even now women make only 72 cents for every dollar made by a man.

Although 75 percent of women work at paid jobs, 40 percent of them earn wages below the poverty level.*

*Paula England, ed., *Comparable Worth: Theories and Evidence* (New York: Aldine de Gruyter, 1992) p. 13.

TEACH EXIT STRATEGIES

She's in high school and is beginning to feel the strain of keeping up with her customers, her schoolwork, and her social life at the same time. Or she borrowed $100 from her grandmother to start a T-shirt business and now, tired of the business, she wants out. But she still owes Gram $50. How do you help her take a different path while honoring commitments and responsibilities?

Help her out by raising the issue and discussing alternatives: hiring help (even if it means losing her own "salary" for a while), selling the business, or negotiating with a competitor to get a percentage of revenues from referrals. Maybe she works off the money she owes her grandmother in another way (housecleaning for a month?). Introduce the concept of an "exit strategy" as a responsible way to change one's mind, as well as a plan for getting out of a business with a profit. And next time she borrows money or starts a business, help her think through an exit strategy BEFORE she gets started.

The idea of a Global Fund for Women came out of a dinner conversation among three women attending a conference in 1987. Ann Firth Murray then took the initiative to gather support and the Fund was created "to assist women in becoming full partners in their societies."

"In every country in the world women are treated unequally in every way. . . . They grow more than half the world's food and own only one percent of the land. And they provide more health care for their families than all health care professionals combined, yet they suffer disproportionately from preventable illnesses," Murray notes. *

Since 1987 the fund has made 677 grants to 533 women's groups in 100 countries to help women develop their own health, safety, and education systems. Among the programs they support are the Colectivo Mujer; Salud y Medicina Social COMUSAMS, a Chilean organization that organizes training and research in women's reproductive health and sexual violence; the Women for Social Progress in Mongolia; and the Female Forum in the Czech Republic.

Murray saw her venture as an entrepreneurial undertaking from the start. The imperative to state your vision, engage others to work with you to realize it, and then find ways to sustain it is no less compelling in the nonprofit world as it is in the private sector. In 1992 Anne was nominated for the California Entrepreneur of the Year Award.

*Daphne White, "A Woman of Conscience," *Foundation News,* Jan.–Feb. 1993, p. 26.

TEACH BIZ VOCABULARY

One way to exclude girls from the financial systems that affect their lives is to keep the language of money and finance a mystery to them. Play a vocabulary game that introduces words associated with money and the management of it. (*Capital, exit strategy, barter, profit,* etc., are all used in this book. If you don't know the language yourself, you can learn together. Use the vocabulary list in the appendix as a starting point.)

Choose three words a week and see how many times she can use the word or the phrase in a sentence that adds understanding to that word. Pay a nickel (or a penny, if she really gets good!) for each time the word is used properly in a sentence. Play Scrabble using financial words for extra points. Start a story on a sheet of paper and stick it on the refrigerator or the class bulletin board; keep the story running by working words and ideas related to money and finances into the narrative. For example:

Marisela wanted to start a bike repair business. She needed *start-up capital* of about $100. Fortunately, she had six cousins who she thought might be willing *investors.* But before writing a *business plan* for them to review, she gave some thought to her *marketing* plan and worked out her *cash flow* needs for six months. What exactly did Marisela do to prepare for her bike repair business?

Rachel Reif and Margaret Kowalsky were winners of the 1993 AIOHO Business Plan Competition. When asked at the awards ceremony why they had entered the competition, Margaret replied, "The first year we started our business"—they were juniors in high school when they opened FUNdamentals, a summer soccer camp for little girls—"it all went really well. But the next year the camp grew—and it got REAL confusing. We saw the ad for the business plan competition and thought it might help—and it did!"

The two young women started FUNdamentals because they played soccer and were dismayed to discover that as they got older, the level of competition they faced seemed to decline. Realizing girls often don't get the coaching necessary to support great competition, Rachel and Margaret took matters into their own hands. Three summers old, the company has to evolve to accommodate the changes in their lives since the two young women, best friends since grade school, are now going to college on opposite sides of the country. And both young women, and the little girls they served, have grown in ways they could not have imagined when the idea first hit.

UNIT 32

PARTNER AN ENTERPRISE

Invite a girl to become your partner in a summer project: growing a garden and selling your produce at the local farmer's market; collecting goods from other people's spring cleaning efforts to hold a giant yard sale; running a birthday cake business for the summer.

You put up the initial cash for seed or materials needed for the project; she offers "sweat equity." That is, if you put $50 into the cost of seeds, she could weed for 5 hours more than you do at $5 per hour to work off her share of the seed money. Make sure you both know the costs (include fertilizer and water, as well as adding a price to your labor) and income (will you charge per tomato or per pound?) and share the profits according to whatever initial plan you agreed to (is it your property? do you get an extra 10 percent for the use of your land?). Keep this first venture small. And don't forget roles—will one of you be the gardener and one be the marketer? Will you both sell at the Farmer's Market? Does one keep business records and the other keep garden records?

At the end of the summer, review together what you learned and what you might do differently next year. Or maybe you have a new business idea in mind!

*Women hold patents on over 5 percent of all inventions and, thanks to the work of the American Association of University Women, Girls Incorporated, Girl Scouts of the USA, and the YWCA, organizations committed to increasing the participation of girls in math and science, we can look forward to an increase in those numbers in the coming years.**

*Ann MacDonald, *Feminine Ingenuity* (New York: Ballantine Books, 1992), p. 379.

PLAY THE STOCK MARKET

Buy play money and give yourself and a young woman $1,000 each. Introduce her to the stock market section of the newspaper. Help her locate several companies she may be familiar with—Ben & Jerry's Homemade Inc.; Mattel, the makers of Barbie (she needs to understand what a big business Barbie commands); and Apple Computer are a few she will probably know.

Use the play money to "invest" in one or more of the companies she is interested in. Watch the stock over time. On the first day of each month, have a "reckoning." When it goes up, give her the "dollars" that reflect the increase in her investment. When the stock drops, take away dollars. Find ways to learn more about the companies you are following. Write and ask for copies of their annual reports, and go over them with her. Keep track of net gains and losses per month, per quarter, per year. Discuss the difference in judging a company by their quarterly performance and by longer term measures.

After you've both gained some confidence, try investing for real!

Marilyn Hamilton once skied down mountains at break-neck speeds. Then, at the age of twenty-nine, she was para-lyzed for life in a hang-gliding accident. Completing rehab therapy in record time, she became immensely frustrated with the wheelchairs available to her—all heavy and hard to maneuver. Familiar with the new materials athletes used in their equipment, Marilyn convinced a couple of her friends to build an ultra-light wheelchair for her. The one they invented was half the weight of existing models. The design was a hit with wheelchair athletes and others who wanted an alternative to the heavier chairs they had been using. With colors in bright purple and neon pink, the sleekly designed chairs helped their owners feel better about themselves.

Quickie Designs now generates about $65 million in annual sales and employs over 400 people. But reinventing the wheel (chair) and building a company was not enough for this strong dreamer. Now the head of marketing for the company she sold to Sunrise Manufacturing—to give Quickie the needed resources to grow—Marilyn has also established Winners on Wheels (WOW), a nonprofit company designed to "empower youth in wheelchairs to be all that they can be." For more information on Quickie and WOW call 209-292-2171.

CALCULATE KID COSTS

Quite appropriately we communicate the joys of having children—someday. But we don't always give practical information to go with the romance involved with the birth of babies. Sit with her and calculate the costs of having a baby—with and without insurance. Figure costs from birth to age eighteen. Include:

Health care—before and after birth (doctors, dentists, specialists)

Food (for the child and some of her friends when she's older)

Clothing (diapers and baby clothes, Reeboks and T-shirts, prom dresses and school clothes)

Toys

Housing

Education

Baby-sitters/Daycare

Entertainment (movies, sports tickets, concerts)

Summer camp or special activities

Equipment (computers, Walkmans, video games)

When you've tallied the numbers discuss how you reached those sums and what it means for the kind of income required to support children.

In 1985 Wilma Mankiller became Principal Chief of the Cherokee Nation, the first woman to hold the post. This achievement was perhaps a natural chapter for the woman who had pursued social justice and economic self-determination for indigenous peoples—as well as herself—all her life.

In 1981 she helped found the Cherokee Nation Community Development Department. The organization sought ways to implement renewal projects in rural Cherokee communities. One of the most cherished achievements of that time was the Bell Project. Bell, Oklahoma, was a poor community with a population of 350 people, 95 percent of whom were Cherokee. A quarter of the people living in Bell had to haul water for household use, and almost half the homes fell below minimum housing standards. Young people left the community to go elsewhere. Bell could have become a ghost town.

Instead, a new water system was installed by community volunteers, bringing the first running water to the town. Twenty homes and the community center were rehabilitated by the townspeople themselves. Twenty-five energy-efficient homes were constructed—again with the townspeople acting as their own labor force. This triumphant form of self-help validated many of the beliefs that the woman who would be chief held about the Cherokees. Interdependence and a willingness to pitch in had saved the community. "Where everyone expected failure, self-help brought success," she states with pride.*

*Wilma Mankiller, Mankiller: A Chief and Her People (New York: St. Martin's Press, 1993), p. 234.

UNIT 35

TAX INFO FOR GIRLS

What are taxes and what difference do they make to her? Most kids know that they cause a lot of anxiety and stress in the family. And whatever taxes are, a teen's natural reaction may be, "They aren't good, but they don't have anything to do with me."

Next time you buy school clothes with a girl, point out the number that is the sales tax on the bill (if you have it in your state). Work with her to find out what taxes support in your state (or local community). Ask her to list the five things she would like her tax money to support. Have her write a letter to her state legislators explaining what she thinks should be covered by the tax—or not. If she gets a paycheck, explain the amount of money that is deducted for income taxes. Suggest she find out what portion of taxes goes to pay for things she cares about, as well as to those things she doesn't want to support.

Make sure she hears you asking questions about what portion of our taxes benefit women and girls. And talk with her about what she can do if she doesn't like the way tax dollars are spent (refer back to Unit 21, VOTE!)

Women now own more than 33 percent of all businesses.*
The next generation may push that to 50 percent!

*National Foundation for Women Business Owners, "The New Economic Work Force," Data Report (Washington, D.C.), (1992), p. 3.

UNIT 36

- - - - - - - - - - - - - - - -

CAREER COACH WITH THE CLASSIFIEDS

Using the classified section of the Sunday paper, ask her to circle six jobs that sound especially interesting. Suggest she write a letter, as if she were twenty-five years old, describing why she's interested in each job and what her qualifications for that job are. A "fill-in-the blanks" sample might look as follows:

Dear Company,

I saw your ad for _____ in the newspaper and wish to apply for the job. I am interested because_____

_____.

Experiences I have had since high school that I think have helped me prepare for the job include_____

_____

_____.

The qualities I possess that would make me most effective include_____

_____

_____.

Though you did not give a firm salary guideline, I would expect to be paid_____. After doing this job for_____[period of time], I plan to_____

_____.

I look forward to talking with you further about your company needs and my career goals.

Sincerely,

Giant's Barber Shop is not just a place to get one's hair cut, it's also an informal meeting place for the African-American community in San Jose, California. It's owned by Arlena Jenkins, who has made the shop a "vehicle for getting information out to people."

Jenkins grew up in San Jose, was a leader all through school and attended California State at Hayward. Knowing she was thinking of going to law school, her father convinced her to work at the barber shop "so she could save money for school." But once there she found herself actually running the business as her dad began to ease out of the shop. In 1988 he sold it to her. Now, with the barber shop as a hub for information, congregation, and a good cut, Arlena is increasingly viewed as a critical member of the community.

Ask around town and any number of people will talk, perhaps hopefully, of having her run for political office. But for now, Arlena remains active in the business community. She volunteers her time to a wide range of projects and issues; and the barber shop her dad started remains healthy under her management.

HAVE FUN!

All work and no play make Jane a dull girl. As you encourage her to focus on economic responsibility—keep it light, have fun, and remember that attention and respect for her passions, her heart, and her spirit are as important as helping her learn what it means to "operate in the black," "have a positive cash flow," and "save for a rainy day."

Anthropologists have discovered there are three kinds of play: instrumental play (like spelling bees and other contests and games designed to combine learning with fun); real play (anything that is unstructured and self-directed—paper dolls and brainstorming both fall in this category); and illegitimate play (spitballs, for example). When real play is constantly blocked, illegitimate play comes to the fore. But where instrumental play can be combined with "business as usual," humans are able to lighten up and learn in new ways.

Getting *too* serious about economic literacy with the young women in your life could be counterproductive to the very gift you wish for her: empowerment!

Margot Fraser, the CEO of Birkenstock Footprint Sandals, Inc., and the woman who has done more good for feet than perhaps any other person in the country, related a story to a group of young women in San Francisco one night. As a young girl living in Germany during World War II, she once said to her father, "When I grow up I want to become an international merchant and bring pride back to Germany." Her father replied, "Girls can't become international merchants."

"My life took me in a different direction at first," she told the girls, "but years later—guess what—I did become an international merchant after all!"

She is certainly that. Margot discovered the ergonomically designed sandal in 1966 while on a trip to Germany, where they are manufactured. Enduring foot problems of her own at that time, she found them so comfortable that she brought back extra pairs to see if others would buy them. In the first year, 10,000 pairs were sold. Today there are over 80 style and color combinations of the shoe and the business has grown to be a $50 million enterprise serving 2,000 retailers! Birkenstocks are now as likely to be seen on the feet of teens as senior citizens.

- - - - - - - - - - - - - - - - - - -

TEACH CONTRACTING

Oral contracts, a shake of the hand, written documents—these forms of covenant or promise are ways of making commitments. Teach young women to make contracts unapologetically and thoughtfully. Does she need a loan? Put it in writing and talk with her about the responsibilities of signing her name. This is one way of getting her comfortable with legal documents as she grows older. Whether reviewing a lease agreement when she rents her first apartment, signing a contract for the local gym, or agreeing to sell her journal about her trip to Patagonia to a publisher, she will need to be cognizant of the possibilities and pitfalls of contracts.

Start with simple contracts (perhaps spelling out a connection between doing chores and her allowance). Make sure some of the contracts you make with her are in writing and others are verbal. Discuss the difference. You don't want to turn family life into one long litigation just to teach a lesson; you do want to introduce the concept of commitment, obligations, and clarity!

*Nationally, the success rate for businesses owned by women is almost twice as high as it is for all businesses.**

*Wisconsin Dept. of Development, "A Report on Women-Owned Businesses," (Madison, Wisconsin: 1991).

CHECKBOOKS

One dirty little secret kept by too many women is that they do not balance their checkbooks. There are, no doubt, myriad good reasons for this (not the least of which is the absence of a book like *No More Frogs to Kiss* for the women who were raising us!). But it's not a good practice to perpetuate into the next generation. Get her started on a checkbook and make sure she balances it regularly. (This is also a good way to reinforce her math competence and self-esteem.) Consider giving incentives if necessary—a balanced checkbook is at least as great an achievement as good grades or a championship run down a steep mountain. Praise her and let her know this is a skill she can master and take pleasure in.

If she has a computer and can afford one of the software programs that handle checking accounts, that's fine. The point is not to make the task difficult, but to get it done.

*In 1967 Muriel Siebert became the first woman to buy a
seat on the New York Stock Exchange. In 1975 she was the
first to sell stocks at a discount. And in 1977 she was
appointed New York State's first woman superintendent of
banking. These accomplishments are part of what made
possible the establishment of the Siebert Entrepreneurial
Philanthropic Plan (SEPP) through which she donates half
of the selling commission on new security underwritings to
charities with the issuer or purchaser choosing the charity.*

*Siebert says she got the idea for SEPP on her birthday in
1990. She attended a luncheon in Manhattan honoring
people who had made contributions to the city. Touched by
the commitment and effort of people being awarded, she
pledged the profits of a bond sale to one of the groups honored. That was the beginning. And as she says, "This is
something that's important to me—but I also want it to
stand as a challenge to others to follow."**

*Since SEPP was established, more than $3.3 million has
been distributed among grassroots groups and other organizations. And in 1993 she established the Los Angeles
Women's Entrepreneurial Fund to help women whose businesses were destroyed in the events following the first ver-
dict related to the beating of Rodney King.*

---

*Beverly Kempton, "What Does Success Really Mean,"
Executive Female, Jan.–Feb. 1993, p. 38.

UNIT 40

SAVING AND BRUSHING TEETH

Set up a long-term account with her: a savings account, a mutual fund, or stock portfolio. Teach saving as you would brushing one's teeth: let her know it's a lifelong process and a personal responsibility.

Discuss the kinds of life situations that make an economic cushion important, from the freedom to take an unpopular stand to the ability to be ready for life's surprises—both the good and the bad. Saving should be introduced as a means of opening doors and choices, rather than as something that prevents her from buying the latest CD! Brainstorm with her on ways to contribute regularly to the account. Suggest she interview friends and adults she respects for ideas about how to create and manage a lifelong savings account.

PART 2

THINGS TO DO IN YOUR COMMUNITY

Both small and grand gestures are required to give girls access to the knowledge, the support, and the resources of our communities. We must invent ways to send a loud, repetitive, and profound message to girls that a) they are important, they count, their ideas and feelings are valid and valuable; and b) we need them as vital, competent, and contributing members of our communities.

Each of the ideas in this section is intended to help you build a girl-friendly community in which young women can acquire language, skills, and experiences aimed at strengthening economic literacy and supporting their entrepreneurial spirit.

Whether it's organizing your neighbors, talking to the mayor, meeting with teachers, or planting seeds that will be harvested as tomorrow's ideas, you can have an impact in your community. At AIOHO we have seen that one person can—and often does—make a difference. Whether you live in a central city, an isolated rural area, or a large suburban community, the girls there need your support and concern. Help make it a place where raising young women to be economically knowledgeable and self-sustaining is not grounds for exile!

Kathy Taggeres is a daring risk-taker. In 1987 she negotiated to purchase Bob's Big Boy Salad Dressing from Marriott Corporation. "I had no money at the time and I had always worked for somebody else. I had to convince Marriott to sell to me. I finally cut a deal to delay payment on a big portion of the cash. I sold everything I had, jewelry, stocks, everything, and got an $800,000 loan from a bank."

In 1988 Taggeres expanded her business, buying a bakery and establishing a pizza line. Her latest venture is KT Kitchens International—a new concept combining technology with food. Taggeres's partner in this venture is Charlene Ondek, an engineer and inventor who founded Ventron, a new high-tech vending machine. Ondek developed the machine to dispense Kathy's frozen pizzas, which are then heated in a microwave built into the unit. Taggeres sells the units to owners of small businesses for placement in lobbies, bars, and school campuses.

The next vision in sight: an automated restaurant in New York City that she describes as a twenty-first-century version of the old Automat.

UNIT 41

TEEN NIGHT AT THE CHAMBER

Start a campaign to sponsor "teen nights" at the Chamber of Commerce, Rotary, and business and professional women's clubs, etc. Each organization can agree to cover a different theme throughout the year: one could have a panel of teen entrepreneurs tell about their businesses; another could explain how kids can obtain licenses and permits to sell products or start small ventures; still another might have a panel of adults talk about their careers and answer questions for teens.

In this way, teens become visible to the business community, and in turn the business community becomes accessible to teens. Their economic development represents an integrated part of the community's obligation to young people, rather than the intrusions of brash young people who haven't learned their "place" in the community. Bridging the generation gap is in part a simple matter of bringing different age groups together. And including young people in the economic web of the community will have long-term benefits for all.

━━ ━━ ━━ ━━ ━━ ━━ ━━ ━━ ━━ ━━ ━━ ━━ ━━ ━━

Of the $2.5 billion in private venture capital invested in 1992, less than 1 percent went to women.*

*"What Do Venture Capitalists Want?" *Women's Business Exclusive,* 2(4), June 1994, p. 6.

UNIT 42

ECONOMIC LITERACY IN THE CLASSROOM

Call a local school administrator or teacher and ask how economic literacy is taught in the classroom. Ask if you can observe classes—talk with girls to find out what they are learning. If you don't think the program is giving girls skills to handle their own economic lives, offer to work with the school to develop a community based after-school program. A list of programs and resources at the back of this book will help. (One caution: kids are not miniature adults for whom diluted MBA courses will work. The success of economic literacy in schools is tied to kid-friendly curricula and engaging activities.)

Sue Scott is an artist who created two multimillion-dollar companies: Primal Lite and Primal Design. Consider her conference table: large, functional, shaped like a trout. Since Scott transforms basic Christmas lights into illuminated lizards, tropical fish, and cacti, it's not surprising to see that she has transformed almost everything else around her—including the rules of business. "When I started I didn't know the rules," she says, "so I didn't know I was breaking them. Tell me what I can't do, and I'll do it," she adds. (A not uncommon statement shared by many entrepreneurs.)

Sue started her business with a plan to make and market a "Lumasaurus," a lamp in the shape of a stegosaurus. But when neither banks nor customers were sold on the idea, she literally went back to the drawing board. Undaunted—and overstocked—Sue returned to the images that had been important to her growing up in the Southwest—the trout and the lizard. She turned them into Christmas lights, and they hit the stores and sold out. One woman wrote to Sue and told her she used them in her garden to keep deer out; others use them in more conventional ways as nightlights and party decorations.

The success inspired Scott to keep on creating. Described as a woman with a "quick wit and a quick mind" by one of her consultants, the woman who recovered from the Lumasaurus is now set to use her talents to realize another vision: "Coming up with designs is easy," she says breezily. "Building a company to support your idea is when the hard work begins."

UNIT 43

SET UP A COMMUNITY MENTORS BANK

How did you learn about economics and money? Chances are that unless you consciously sought out classes or training, much of your information came from someone "showing you the ropes."

Many communities now have mentoring programs—either as part of a community group or a school program. If there is one, join it—and make sure a girl you know is able to take advantage of it. If there isn't one, be a gadfly and get a program going in your town. Make sure some portion of the program emphasizes economic literacy.

We recommend experience based programs—that is, programs offering a set of experiences or activities that help girls build skills as well as relationships. Building relationships with adults is important and desirable, but unless those relationships are augmented by the opportunity to share real experiences, girls may feel good but leave the program no more economically literate than when they started.

Annette Taylor, Susan Davis, Judith Luther Wilder, and Lindsey Johnson are committed to creating funds—and providing access to capital—that allow women to expand their companies. Maxing out credit cards, borrowing from family, bartering, and bootstrapping have been the means women have employed to start their companies—with good results. But money to help those companies grow has been scarce.

Annette started the Women's Equity Fund (303-443-2620) in Colorado. She invests from $10,000 to $100,000 in service, retail, and light manufacturing businesses, a different strategy than that pursued by most venture companies, which aim to loan $1 million and up, banking on a big return. Susan Davis started Capital Circle (708-876-1101) with the intention of getting "all the players in a room together." Her notion that access to money is a function of access to the network that controls money is behind the forums she creates for women to present their business plans to potential funders. And Judith Luther Wilder and Lindsey Johnson teamed up to create Women, Inc. (916-448-8444), a venture to provide new credit tools that will facilitate women's access to capital. Their goal is to provide access to a loan pool of $30 million for women business owners around the country.

These companies are a bridge between micro-lending and more conventional venture capital. Taylor, Davis, Wilder, and Johnson demonstrate the importance of women investing in other women. As more women follow their lead, women's businesses will continue to grow into the twenty-first century.

KNOWLEDGE IS POWER

Prepare a reading list related to money and business for girls (steal the list at the back of this book if you like) and make it available to community leaders, educators, and parents through PTAs or other community organizations.

Although there are more pamphlets and books related to drug abuse, pregnancy, and domestic violence available to girls now, we still don't make it easy for them to find out about issues related to money and economic well-being.

Put it in a plain brown wrapper if you think that will make the list more interesting!

The Department of Labor estimates that 44 percent of workers who become unemployed will need retraining to find work. All the more reason to help teen women learn how to "make a job" as a way of establishing economic security.

UNIT 45

BROWN BAG LUNCHES

Set up a series of brown bag lunches for girls at a local school. Devote each lunch to a different topic: careers, money, economics. After the first couple of sessions, ask the girls to help set the topic. Many girls have questions about paying for school, getting into college, getting jobs, etc., and no clear place to get answers to their questions. Even if you don't know the answers, you can work with them on ways to get them. Some of the questions we have found provocative and that help get girls talking include:

How do you think you'll take care of yourself when you're older?

How did your mother and your grandmother handle money, and will money be different or the same for you?

How can your dreams help you buy a house, raise a family, pay bills?

What comes to mind when someone mentions the word *business*?

What is your family's attitude about money and how does that affect you?

Susan Gubitosa grins when she says, "In my high school year-book I was called a space cadet, no one would have thought I'd run my own business!" The Neon Factory in New Jersey is Susan's business and she runs it with the self-confidence that comes with exploring many other paths before finding the one right for her. "I was a fitness instructor," she says, "and then I traded commodities.

"Finally, my stepfather suggested that I learn his trade: glass blowing. I had nothing to lose and it turned out I had a talent for it. So I set up a workshop, printed stationery, and opened my business with a party—the problem was that no one came— that was my first lesson in the value of marketing!"

Today Susan's company services customers in retail, design, and construction. And she balances her quest for economic growth with her commitment to giving back to girls. Because she understands the importance of guidance at a young age, she regularly spends time with a Girl Scout troop near her home. She is also a coach for a young entre-preneur who probably won't be called a "space cadet" in her *yearbook!*

SMALL BUSINESS INTERNSHIPS

Many businesses would welcome young women as interns for a period of time—to learn about the business, to observe people at work, to develop skills such as computer literacy and the ability to get a task done. But the time or experience to set up a program that matches girls with projects that need to be done or supervisors who can oversee the assignment is scarce.

Set up an internship program in your community. Try to arrange a partnership among local businesses that will provide intern "slots," find community organizations that will make the program known to girls, and start a local foundation that will pay for computer support, telephone costs, and other administrative requirements for running such a program.

Make each internship a three- to six-month assignment. This is meant as a learning experience for girls that gives businesses a couple of extra hands for short periods in exchange for exposing girls to the world of business. Make sure it doesn't become just a free labor pool for businesses!

Dolores Ratcliffe started Corita Communications after almost a dozen years as a teacher. Corita is a consulting firm that specializes in technical and educational assistance. But after running her company for a few years, she felt the need for an organization that would connect and support black women entrepreneurs. Not a woman to wait for "someone else" to fix things, Ratcliffe established the Association of Black Women Entrepreneurs, a national organization based in Los Angeles that offers training, referral networks, and a support system to black women who are starting businesses as well as those who have been at it for a while.

In 1987 Dolores also published a business survival guide called Women Entrepreneurs, Networking, and Sweet Potato Pie *(we can attest to the excellence of the pie!). The book is based on real experiences of women who have started companies and is intended for the person who already has an idea in mind and is ready to "get to work." For information on both the book and the organization, call 213-624-8639.*

CREATE A SPEAKERS' BUREAU FOR GIRLS' ISSUES

You remember how jazzed you got when you heard one of your sheros* speak, right? Well, think about what it might mean to girls to hear a steady stream of women over the course of a school year tell stories about careers, business, money, and economics (as well as the arts, adventure, politics, and sports). Arrange with local schools—or after-school programs—to set up a program and supply them with a series of speakers who will reliably show up and spend a half-hour talking to girls. (Less is more—don't let adults drone on to the MTV Generation!)

Ask each speaker to make a school-work connection somewhere in her talk and make sure the girls have time to ask questions. Include women of diverse backgrounds, class, culture, and race; recognize different kinds of success. Create a variety of formats: a panel discussion, an "Oprah"-like question and answer session, small group discussions that begin with one woman telling her story for fifteen minutes. Ask the young women how they would like to see some of the talks structured.

*Thank you, Alice Walker!

A survey conducted by Women in Philanthropy and the Boston Women's Fund in 1993 found that 61 percent of grant funders believe there are no particular obstacles to funding programs for girls. Sixty-three percent of programs for women and girls believe they have less chance of being funded because of their focus. Sixty-eight percent of philanthropic board members are male; 89 percent are white. *

*Molly Mead, *Worlds Apart* (Women in Philanthropy and the Boston Women's Fund, 1994), p. 8.

PARTIES LTD.

Invite a group of adults to contract for a series of parties. Ask teams of two to four girls, drawn from a local girls club or school, to participate by giving each team a "party contract" to fulfill. A contract card gives the age group, the number of people, and the budget that each "client" wants her Parties Ltd. team to produce.

Each team has a week to work out location, food, entertainment, etc., based on the specifications of the client. The team's goal is to produce a great party, stay on budget, *and make a profit*. Girls make their presentations at a luncheon with the "contractors" and vote for the party they would most like to attend.

Explore the experience with the girls and have them talk about how they worked together, how they did their research, what they enjoyed about the process, and what they might do differently next time.

Gun Denhart and her husband, Tom, started the Hanna Andersson catalog to offer soft cotton children's clothes that were imported from Gun's native Sweden. The clothes were durable and fun for kids, and the company became a leader in the movement to combine social values and profit.

One of Gun's best inventions is the Hannadown. Customers are encouraged to return their used clothing for a 20 percent credit on future purchases. Donated clothes are passed along to needy children (particularly those living in emergency conditions, the homeless, and those in shelters due to domestic violence). As of March 1994, the program had generated credits of over $700,000. Hanna Andersson now employs over 270 people and has annual sales of over $44 million. The entire company is committed to creating ways to make the company grow in a way that will demonstrate the integration of concern for community with attention to profits.

UNIT 49

USE THE PRESS!

Talk with local newspapers and television programmers about the possibility of carrying a regular column on economic literacy for kids. (Call it "Econ. Lit for Teens" or "MoneyMakers.")

Perhaps it can go on the comic page, or fill a couple of inches on the business page. Even if kids don't read it regularly, they will be introduced to the topics and language of money and business over time. Teachers can weave the pieces into other class lessons; parents can collect the columns for use at a later time. Almost every community has a few young entrepreneurs. How about a column shared by a teen and an adult entrepreneur?

Frieda, Karen, and Jackie Caplan constitute a produce dynasty. Mother Frieda started Frieda's Finest—selling exotic fruits and vegetables—over twenty-five years ago. Elephant garlic, round carrots, yellow watermelons, and kiwi are just a few of the 400 items this educational entrepreneur brought to your local market. Frieda opened her own wholesale produce outlet in L.A. in 1962 with a $10,000 loan from her father, a Russian immigrant. She became known for stocking "weird stuff" and within a year had repaid the loan.

In 1990 Frieda's daughters bought the company from their mother and eldest daughter Karen became CEO. Karen continued her mom's tradition of staying on the cutting edge. A leader in the field of produce marketing, she was one of the first in the produce industry to institute a Total Quality Management Program. Younger sister Jackie handles key account sales for the company.

The Caplans represent a growing and exciting development in business—companies are changing hands, going from one generation to the next, not just from father to son or daughter now, but from mother *to daughter as well. Both Jackie and Karen have children who may well represent the third generation of this remarkable family of innovative entrepreneurs.*

All the Caplans feel strongly about the importance of investing in women. Not only do they make regular contributions to a variety of women's funds, they also support scholarships for girls to pursue careers in agriculture.

UNIT 50

------- ------ ------ ------ ------ ------ ------ ------ ------ ------ ------

START—OR ADD TO—A FUND FOR GIRLS

Now there's a radical idea! Just a fraction of all foundation money is currently awarded to programs serving women and girls (under 5 percent). To make funding more equitable, a number of cities (Boston, Kansas City, Mo., San Francisco, and Los Angeles, to name a few) have established foundations that recognize the needs of women and girls.

If your city doesn't have such a fund yet, get one started. Organize the community's women, funding agents, and program executives and start the ball rolling. If you do have a women's foundation in your community, give it a check for the holidays, in celebration of a friend's birthday, or in honor of Women's Suffrage (August 19)! Set an ambitious target. Can you raise a million dollars in your community just for girls' services?

Forty-two percent of women workers earn less than $10,000 annually, compared to 24 percent of male workers.* Operation SMART, *a program started by Girls Incorporated to encourage girls to explore math, science, and technology is one way to change this statistic.*

*Girls Incorporated, *Seeds for Growth: Operation SMART Training Guide*, (New York), p. 3.

CREATE A COMMUNITY TEACH-IN FOR KIDS

Music lessons, art lessons, dance lessons—what about the selling lessons? These days almost every community has a flea market or a farmers' market, or garage sales on the weekend. Create a kids' flea market and kick it off a month before with some lessons on how to sell. Place posters in schools, advertise on the radio, offer to match adults with teens who want help. Make this a flea market run by and for kids.

Adults can provide coaching tips with a flyer or a telephone tip line. Suggest they sell something they no longer use (dolls no longer played with . . . a bike no longer in use . . .) or encourage them to make something they think there's a need for.

Offer a prize for the best sales effort (a combination of factors including revenue, relevance, presentation, ingenuity, etc.). Learning how to sell a product is one way to help young people build confidence. If your daughter sells Girl Scout cookies, this is a perfect opportunity to discuss the importance of introducing herself, building relationships with customers, and listening to what customers need. Explore with her the connections between selling cookies door to door and selling in other venues—like a community flea market.

Shanta is a storyteller entrepreneur who says, "When I was a kid I was always getting in trouble for running off at the mouth. Now I get paid for running my mouth!" Divorced, poor, the mother of three, Shanta enrolled in the Women's Employment Project in Chicago and learned how to manage her storytelling skills as a business.

Now she gets paid to travel and tell stories in schools, onstage, and at conferences. Many of her stories (there are over 150 in her repertoire) come out of African traditions and emphasize self-esteem, courage, voice, peace, and confidence. As the stories are also participatory, children become involved and excited about their own storytelling skills. She often accompanies her stories with sounds from African instruments: the shekere, the African thumb piano, a four-string harp from Kenya, and the reed zither from Nigeria. Sometimes she is accompanied by her daughter, who still giggles at her mother's stories.

In the mid-eighties, Shanta founded Storywiz Records and Services. Now she produces her own CDs and cassettes, making her stories more widely available to children everywhere. For more information about Shanta and her stories, call Artists of Note at 708-557-2742.

CREATE SCHOLARSHIPS

Across race and class, girls need financial assistance to go to college. One of our favorite AIOHO supporters didn't go to college. Though a highly successful business owner now, she remembers that the family didn't have enough money to send her to school and no one encouraged her to apply for scholarships (though her grades were high) or financial assistance. "The subject of college was avoided altogether—I guess they hoped I'd forget about it!"

Create a community scholarship fund that gives girls support for their dreams. Remember that college tuition is just the beginning of the financial responsibilities associated with going to college. For teen moms, an obstacle may be daycare; for physically challenged girls, help with transportation may be important; and former gang members may need support counseling.

While college is no longer a guarantee of economic power, lack of college is still a pretty strong indicator of *less* economic power. If there is no support for a scholarship fund for girls in your community, make sure that the scholarships awarded show gender equity.

About Women, Inc., is the culmination of Janice Leeming's interest in the economic power of women. She was one of the first venture capitalists to see potential in women-owned businesses but had to start her own investment company to make the kinds of investments she believed in. "My male partners rarely took seriously the deals I brought in if they were businesses started by women."

In 1988 Leeming invested in a company that recognized the purchasing power of women. "Women don't influence buying decisions," she points out, "they purchase; 73 to 85 percent of everything, consumer products and services and durable goods as well." When the original founder left, Janice switched her role from investor to CEO. She has spent the last six years building a company that conducts research on women consumers and consults to companies savvy enough to understand the importance of taking women seriously.

The Boston-based firm is one of the first to fearlessly state: Women count and we're going to pay attention to what they do, think, and want. Last year Leeming and company vice president Cynthia Tripp wrote Segmenting the Women's Market. *This guide to the ways women use their economic power is based on the solid research that the company engages in.*

Now running her own company, Leeming maintains she has more fun now than when she invested in others: "This is active, I see the results of my decisions," she says. For information on About Women, Inc., call 617-723-4337.

START A CLUB

Whether it's a monthly session at the local girls club, a potluck dinner once a quarter in the homes of various women, or a weekly meeting at school, provide a space and time for girls to meet and talk about money, finances, business, and dreams. The local club can invite women business owners to speak, create an investment club, teach the use of spread sheets on computers, watch videos about women business owners (see resources, in appendix), explore ethical dilemmas in business, and provide support to young entrepreneurs. For more information on how to start An Income of Her Own Club, call 800-350-2978.

Boys tend to enter paid employment earlier than girls and earn higher rates of pay.

*Carnegie Corporation, "A Matter of Time: Risk and Opportunity in the Non-School Hours" (New York, December 1992), p. 32.

TEACH ADULTS TO EMPOWER TEENS

Most grown-ups want to do something to help kids grow into self-sufficient adults. In partnership with a PTA, local community college, or a bank, organize a workshop for adults working with girls. Use this book as a workshop guide and offer a forum to discuss issues of gender and economic power. Topics for the workshop might include:

Using family finances to teach economic literacy

Gender and money

Resources for parents

Basic language and concepts of economic literacy and
    entrepreneurship for kids

A community plan for kids and economic literacy

After Los Angeles erupted in violence in 1992, teacher Tammy Bird and six of her students created a garden in back of Crenshaw High School's football field. Their initial plan was to grow vegetables and give them away to the needy in South Central Los Angeles. But when the first crop was harvested, Melinda McMullen (a Los Angeles public relations professional who had never been in the inner city before) visited the garden. "Why not try selling the vegetables?" she asked. Her idea was to give the students a feeling of power by giving them a stake in a real business.

It didn't take long for the students to realize that the vegetables they had grown were the basis of a great salad dressing! Food from the 'Hood was born, and their first product, Straight Out 'the Garden is in 2,000 grocery stores in Southern California.

Melinda gave up her executive job to work with the teenage owners of Food from the 'Hood. Tammy Bird, a biology teacher stopped coaching volleyball (she's also a biology teacher at the high school) to have more time for the growing business. They may be "accidental entrepreneurs," but their efforts are helping teenagers channel their energy to make money, have fun, and create a scholarship fund for Crenshaw High students. To learn more about Food from the 'Hood, call 213-295-4842.

UNIT 55

LEND A HAND TO EXISTING ORGANIZATIONS

Many girls clubs, schools, and gender-equity organizations are underfunded and understaffed. Check in with local youth organizations working with girls to find out what they are doing that is related to economic literacy or entrepreneurship education, what they need, and where they can use some help.

Learn about the organization, observe their programs, read their literature. Then offer to help—or set up and find funding for economic empowerment activities—in a way that shows you are committed to helping the organization meet its goals. Write something up for review before getting too far ahead of the organization—make it easy for them to use your help!

Ottawa-born Sheila Cluff was spied by a scout looking for professional ice skaters when she was just sixteen. For the next few years she traveled with young people who made a lot of money (for their age) and "spent it all," she remembers. We had no expenses—room and board were taken care of—so I saved my salary. And since everyone else ran out of money before I did, I loaned them money, charged interest, and in some cases even managed their money for them!"

Sheila was eighteen and in New York—skating in a review at the Roxy Theater. "Those were," she says, "the days of the Stork Club, '21,' the Latin Quarter. I grew up fast." But the sophistication that comes of living in New York and financial acumen were not the only things this enterprising skater was picking up. What Sheila learned about fitness and exercise during that time stayed with her as well. The former skating star (and then talk show host) continued to manage her money and eventually established two spas that cater to people who want affordable fitness with a little pampering. The Palms and The Oaks are retreats in Southern California to which customers return year after year. And though she doesn't manage other people's money any longer, a number of other women entrepreneurs claim that "Sheila got me started." A founding member of the Committee of 200 (a prestigious group of business women), Sheila understands the importance of supporting other entrepreneurs.

RUN A BUSINESS PLAN COMPETITION

An Income of Her Own runs the National Business Plan Competition annually (call 800-350-2978 for applications). Independent of, or in conjunction with, this national contest, set up a local competition with judges, prizes, and support. Harvard Business School professor Rosabeth Moss Kantor reminds us that in any competition, attention should be paid not just to winners, but to all the kids who have the initiative to participate. At AIOHO we try to match runners-up with coaches for the next year's competition.

Decide in advance what your definition of success is. We don't require applicants to *start* the businesses they write plans for, only that they show imagination, good research, sound thinking, and a plan for a profit. We also encourage young people to work in partnership, since that's a great opportunity to learn the value—and the challenges of—teamwork in a low-risk environment. Make sure you have teen women among your competition's judges' panel.

*"More than 90 percent of girls between 3–10 have a Barbie. . . .
Mattel spends in the neighborhood of $20 million to announce
each addition to the Barbie line."*

*Selina Guber and Jan Berry, *Marketing to and Through Kids*
(New York: McGraw Hill, 1993), pp. 70, 129.

ADOPT A CLASS

The Have a Dream Foundation was one of the first "adopt-a-class" programs. In that program, an entrepreneur concerned about the nation's youth pledged to send the whole class to college if they stayed in school. You may not have the resources to do that, but you may be able to enrich a class in a more modest way. Consider one of these ideas (and convince your friends to make pledges of their own):

Provide the class with a subscription to one or more magazines that deal with teens and business. (See appendix for suggestions.)

Help stock the classroom library with appropriate books and magazines.

Each calendar quarter, arrange for business leaders—entrepreneurs, investors, bankers, inventors, and scientists—or business reporters to talk about some aspect of finance, money, business. (Make sure they are engaging and enjoy young people!)

Donate videos of women business owners and issues related to business, games, or software that can be used by students

Set up a "Gender-Equity Materials Fund," a pool of money that can be tapped to purchase materials not otherwise affordable, for teachers.

In 1979, anticipating the opportunities of the new mobile workforce, Patty DeDominic founded PDQ Personnel Services, Inc. Today PDQ has revenues of over $15 million annually and Patty looks at both the Pacific Rim and the growing Hispanic community in Los Angeles as areas for her company to grow. She describes her company as "a supermarket of skills," a resource to which both large and small companies can turn to obtain skilled people for as long or as short a time as necessary. She wanted to start a staffing company that listened carefully to job seekers' needs. In giving former full-time employees a vehicle for steady employment, PDQ eases some of the disjuncture caused by the structural changes in the economy.

Long active in the National Association of Women Business Owners, Patty recently served a term as the national president. During her term she increased membership, expanded the use of technology to provide resources for women business owners, and created partnerships with organizations that extend information and benefits to NAWBO members. A woman with a global perspective, she was recently elected to a three-year term representing all U.S. women business owners in the worldwide organization, Les Femmes Chefs d'Entreprises Mondiales.

UNIT 58

AUDIT YOUR LOCAL PHILANTHROPIES

It used to be that Boy Scouts routinely received ten times the support from community funds than did Girl Scouts. That disparity has lessened in recent years and the average difference is now around 50 percent more funding in many communities. Change in the funding priorities of local philanthropic organizations is usually a result of citizen involvement and education.

Before making out your annual check to the community fund or a local charity, ask for a report that details money specifically given to girls. By constant, repetitive attention to this issue, the San Francisco Women's Foundation moved community givers to increase their allocations from 1 percent of all grant money awarded to 5 percent. Obviously their work is not done, but that kind of watchdog attention is what will be required for changing funding habits all over the country.

Cruz Hernandez Otazo is nicknamed "Cookie," but she gives Debbie Fields no competition! For many years she ran a highly successful daycare center in Florida. Then the business her husband, Julio, owned was restructured and she decided to become its managing partner. MCO Environmental, Inc., specializes in environmental construction: asbestos abatement, lead-based paint abatement, and radon mitigation are just a few of the areas that Cookie targeted for company growth.

She describes her enterprise as a "medium-sized company in a high-risk business." In 1992 she was elected the first woman director of the Hispanic-American Builders Association. When she first took over the management of MCO Environmental, she says, one problem was that she was known as Julio's wife. Now, she laughs, "he is often referred to as Cookie's husband!"

SEEK LOST GIRLS

Girls on probation, in programs for teen mothers, in homeless shelters, or sanctuaries from domestic violence have the same needs for support, self-esteem, and social inclusion as the girls you will meet in after-school clubs and at school. But often they are invisible, lost in a system without enough resources, time, and energy to seek them out and offer access to experiences and opportunities that could help them develop their own economic safety net.

Whatever else you do, always make sure you include these young women in programming plans and activities. Poverty among women in America is often a function of situation—divorce, widowhood, the loss of a job, illness. Economic vulnerability among girls is especially acute for the most invisible among us. Remember them and reach out.

The poverty rate for women is about 35 percent higher for older women than older men. About 25 percent of older women can expect to be poor in their old age.*

*Jo Ann Lordahl, *Money Meditations for Women* (Berkeley, California: Celestial Arts, 1994), p. 84.

UNIT 60

USE YOUR LIBRARIES!

Andrew Carnegie was one of the first entrepreneurs to understand the role of the library in public education. Work with the public libraries in your area to publish a reading list for teen entrepreneurs. Ask them to post the list at the library entrance and set up a special shelf for recommended books and magazines related to kids and money. Give them a copy of the resource list in the back of this book, help them identify "sponsors" to help purchase items on the list. In light of the cutbacks so many public libraries are experiencing these days, make sure you support them and, if necessary, help set up a special fund for the purchase of materials and books for young entrepreneurs. Offer to run a special "reading circle" that focuses on the economic empowerment of girls—historic and current.

PART 3

THINGS TO DO IN YOUR COMPANY

The editor of *Inc.* magazine, George Gendron, maintains that business owners are among the country's most optimistic people—"They *must* be, to keep taking risks with companies," he adds. And we have found that business owners feel a special desire to share the entrepreneurial spirit and teach economic literacy to young people.

IBM wants future employees who can initiate ideas, anticipate needs, and operate with more entrepreneurial values. Companies like Ben & Jerry's Homemade, Inc., want to support the next generation's awareness of social justice and environmental issues by encouraging young entrepreneurs to invent new kinds of businesses. MCI executives support programs for young people because they believe those who learn entrepreneurial skills at an earlier age will be knowledgeable customers in the Information Age. Most of the businesswomen we know want to share information and skills with young women that earlier generations of women were denied. And almost all business owners understand that a healthy business environment that engages young people is an important ingredient in the health of the larger community.

We understand that many companies will be reluctant to do something "just for girls" and will opt for coed programs instead. If that is the course chosen, we urge you to set aside some part of the program for girls only. The developmental needs of boys and girls are different at this age and one way to meet those needs is to provide gender-specific programming. Women role models and attention to the values and concerns of women and girls are too often missing from so-called coed programs.

The suggestions that follow are intended as a "bridge" between girls and businesses. Try them out; share with us other activities you have tried, and in the next edition of *No More Frogs to Kiss* we'll share them with others.

Twelve years ago, Ella Williams was scrounging aluminum cans from dumpsters to raise milk money for her children. Today she is the president and CEO of her company, Aegir Systems, a nationally recognized engineering and computer services company.

While raising two daughters, Ella pursued a degree and worked in traditional "women's jobs." But after her marriage ended, she was concerned that a secretary's salary would not enable her to give her children the education she wanted for them. Parlaying the skills she developed as an accounting assistant at Hughes Aircraft, she decided to start her own business in the aerospace field. Finally, after three years of tenacious relationship building and proposal writing, Ella got her first contract—$8 million with the Pacific Missile Test Center at Point Mogu, California. Many contracts and almost ten years later, Ella won Outstanding Small Business Contractor of the Year and Small Business Prime Contractor of the Year awards from the Small Business Administration. Her company is now involved in quality-control testing for the new Los Angeles Metro System.

Her most recent venture is Ella's World Class Cheesecakes, Breads, and Muffins, a business established to create jobs for inner-city youth in Los Angeles. Ella's vision: to provide college scholarships for 100 minority youths.

GIVE AWAY A MANAGER

Loan an executive to a nonprofit organization that serves the needs of girls. Grant writers, financial managers, activity leaders, and project managers are all roles that can help advance the goals of local girls organizations. Create a bank of people who may be available for a few hours a week (an accountant who could handle a nonprofit's quarterly reports, for example), a day a week (as a computer instructor for a teen mother's program), or full time for six to twelve months (as a consultant setting up a capital fund for a nonprofit). Send letters to local organizations inviting them to submit a "loaned executive proposal." At Levi Strauss, for example, community involvement teams act together to support specific community projects; at Timberland, employees join members of City Year for a day or a week of community service. Hold a training program for AIOHO activities and give employees and managers time to run those activities in local girls programs or at the company site.

Melissa Grassey, a.k.a. Little Miss Muffin, founded Little Miss Muffin . . . and More, a muffin shop that was the natural outgrowth of a business she started when she was eleven. When she was nine she frequented the local swimming pool. One day she decided the pool needed a snack bar. She went home and worked on a "business plan" for a snack bar. Though that first plan didn't go anywhere (a not unusual fate for first business plans!), it did get her into the entrepreneurial mode of thinking.

A couple of years later when Melissa announced she wanted to go to private school, her mother agreed that "if she could earn the money, she could go." A family friend suggested making something for breakfast that would go with coffee, and Melissa started on a plan to sell muffins. She put on paper what she would need to buy, how much it would cost, and where she could buy her supplies inexpensively. Melissa's determination was enough to get her whole family into the act. Soon Mom was taking orders from Melissa (when she ran out of muffins on her door-to-door route, her mother would jump in the car and replenish the stock). Eventually Melissa's delivery "basket" was replaced by a red wagon and her older brother went along to help with the deliveries.

At thirteen, Melissa became the youngest member of her local Chamber of Commerce. And not long after that she opened a bake shop.

In April 1994 Melissa sold Little Miss Muffin so she could concentrate full time on college. We don't know what her next adventure will be, but she thinks the learning that she experienced with her muffin business will be important no matter what she does.

------- ------- ------- ------- ------- ------- --

CREATE INFORMATION SUPERHIGHWAY STATIONS FOR TEENS

Set up "information entrance ramps" for kids—and make sure that at least part of the time is officially reserved for girls only. Though schools are doing their best to introduce young people to the information super-highway, there aren't enough computers or teachers or "plugged-in" schools to prepare the next generation for the competitive economic world facing them.

Create a "superhighway station," one or more com-puters that are set aside for a certain number of hours per week or month for young people to use. Invite a local community organization to handle scheduling and supervising of teens on the equipment. Make a computer specialist available to teach, answer questions, and help guide young people through an exploration of the "superhighway."

About 40 percent of adolescents' waking hours are discretionary—not filled with eating, school, homework, chores, or working for pay.* That means there is time to build in activities that develop economic literacy!

*Carnegie Corporation, "A Matter of Time: Risk and Opportunity in the Non-School Hours" (New York, December 1992), p. 28.

UNIT 63

MAKE TAKE OUR DAUGHTERS TO WORK DAY WORK

You've decided to participate in the annual Take Our Daughters to Work Day (or have scheduled one of your own). Now what are you going to do? Here are a few suggestions:

1. Establish your goals: a program for the kids of employees? Awareness building for a local school group? The start of a long-term relationship with one or more girls? Different goals will lead to different programs for the day.

2. Convene a group of young women and ask what they would like.

3. Set up a buddy system—match each girl invited with a woman who will be her "guide" for the day. Make sure the "buddy" has a plan and has been coached on the company's goals for the day.

4. Call the Ms. Foundation for Women and ask for its Take Our Daughters to Work organization kit.

5. Host a reception for the teens and invite members of the Committee of 200, National Association of Women Business Owners, the Hispanic Chamber of Commerce, and the Association of Black Women Entrepreneurs or other relevant business organizations in your town.

6. Use the day to announce and launch an ongoing program that engages young women with the company.

7. Make your company a part of the network giving economic power to girls!

Ellen Pack refers to an old joke when describing her decision to start an on-line service for women: "Two shoe salesmen go to a tropical island. One calls his office and says, 'I'm coming back tomorrow—no one here wears shoes.' The other one calls his office and says, 'Don't expect me back for a month, no one here wears shoes yet!'" Ellen Pack and Nancy Rhine have—in metaphorical form—gone to the island. Less than 15 percent of Internet users are women and the conventional wisdom is that women aren't sufficiently interested in technology to crowd the information superhighway. Convinced that women must be citizens of cyberspace to be fully competitive and part of the information revolution, and that the numbers will grow in time, Pack and Rhine officially launched Women's Wire in January of 1994.

The partners hope that a woman-friendly net will tempt women to "wear shoes." And what they have been finding, not surprisingly, is that once women understand the ability to maintain and develop relationships, get feedback, "stay connected" with one another—and get information on everything from childcare to menopause, politics to passions—they will spend more time using it as a means of communication. To learn more about Women's Wire, call 800-210-9999.

UNIT 64

--- --- --- --- --- --- --- --- --- --- --- --- ---

USE YOUR PURCHASING POWER FOR GIRLS

Select one or more girls organizations and augment their budget. You may not be in a position to make generous cash grants, but perhaps you can offer to print their newsletter, or other program needs. Are you making a large purchase of office equipment? Capital items like furniture, copiers, and items you are able to purchase at a considerable discount may be unattainable for programs struggling to meet their budgets. Adopt a girls organization and make an annual "equipment grant." One woman we know provides mailing labels for a nonprofit. It doesn't add much to her company's budget, but it makes a big difference to the girls' program. Request a wish list from a girls organization and get each of your friends to cover one of the items on the list.

Men. Blue suits. Coffee.

(Source: Jamila Hubbard, 18,
on the image of business
she had growing up in
Fremont, California).

Fun. Interesting. I'm beginning to realize how much I like money. And that I've got what it takes to earn it.*

(Source: Jamila, on the
image she has now,
after being named a winner
of AIOHO's National
Business Plan Competition
for Teens and meeting some
of the nation's leading business
women. Jamila's entry detailed
the start-up of a business that
designed clothes for tall teens.
When asked if she also would
design clothes specifically for
short girls, Jamila, six feet tall herself,
replied, "Probably not. I never had
that problem.")

**Inc.*, *16*(7), July 1994, p. 9.

EDUCATE YOUR TRADE ASSOCIATION

Next time you are asked to suggest a topic for your industry's convention suggest that "The Future of Girls" be a topic. Share a copy of the study published by the American Association of University Women (call 202-785-7700 for a copy), "How Schools Shortchange Girls," and make it clear that the future of girls is an economic issue for all businesses. Invite experts on the topic to address your association conference (leaders of girls organizations, advocacy groups, and leading educational centers will be happy to address this topic).

Only when business leaders are educated about the rewards of attending to the future of girls will we see a shift in focus and resources that benefit girls.

Over 23 percent of all black women are huddled together in service positions where the growth in jobs is more impressive than the growth in pay.*

*Cydney Shields and Leslie Shields, *Work, Sister, Work* (New York: Simon & Schuster, 1994), p. 172.

AUDIT YOUR BUSINESS

Examine your company's sponsorships, grant programs, special events, scholarship funds, internships, and other community links and programs. Are your coed efforts really coed? Are girls visible in your efforts? Do they benefit from business grant programs equitably with boys? If not, fix it!

Barbara Thomas started Barbara Thomas Enterprises in 1972. As a medical records administrator, she made the lives of doctors easier with a small but vital invention—a signature marker that was a kind of "medical Post-it, before Post-its were invented." Realizing that what worked for one hospital might work for others, Thomas left her job to start her own company. Selling through direct mail, she became a primary supplier of removable indicator tags for hospitals.

In 1983 daughter Nancy Thomas-Cote took over the helm envisioning a period of growth and expansion for the company. Under her guidance, BTE, Inc., reached beyond medical supplies and offered products to the broader office supply market. Now all the major wholesalers in the industry carry supplies from BTE.

Expanding the company has enabled Barbara and Nancy to fulfill dreams that went beyond creating a comfortable life for themselves and their families. Every year the company now supports scholarships for young women and single parents. Knowing the difference that owning a company of their own has made in their lives, Barbara and Nancy seek ways to help others realize independence through economic control over their lives.

UNIT 67

LEVERAGE IN-HOUSE EDUCATION PROGRAMS

Do you have an in-house training and education department? Use it as a way to extend training programs for local organizations. Set aside a certain number of seats for each class that might be appropriate for a young person. Or maybe your training staff can design an economic literacy program that is appropriate for entry-level employees and teens. Offer a course once, twice, or four times a year that is specifically designed to engage girls in the language and culture of business as well as in the basics of profit, loss, cash management, etc. Partner with a girls' organization to create such a program.

Laura Henderson used every penny of her own savings to start her own biomedical research firm in 1979. Prospect Associates manages national communications projects on topics such as AIDS, cancer, diabetes, Alzheimer's disease, and mental health issues. Their products also include reports, conferences, training programs, exhibits—"thoughtware," as Laura refers to them. Thoughtware, she says, is anything that meets the public health needs of the nation by combining education, technology, and experience.

Thoughtware must work because Laura's company has grown to 150 employees and $10 million in revenues. Appearing on The Oprah Winfrey Show, *Henderson described the start-up of her company as a tremendous dedication to doing research. "Not just reading," she said, "but listening. I had lunch with anyone who would have lunch with me. I talked to anyone who had run a business. I talked to people who I thought had good ideas about running businesses. I also read. But I sought information everywhere I could."*

UNIT 68

OFFER ECONOMIC LITERACY AS A BENEFIT FOR EMPLOYEES' KIDS

Concern for the children of employees helps your business, your employees, the community, and the future. Consider these options:

A newsletter, sent to the home (Turned-On Business or New Moon offer opportunities to create custom newsletters for employee's children; see resources in appendix for contact information)

A video, made available to parents; as a role model story. A video of Susan Gubitosa, profiled earlier, is available

Scholarships, to summer entrepreneurship programs for kids

A training workshop, for parents interested in providing economic literacy projects, programs, and information for their kids.

Offering information, materials, and financial assistance related to economic literacy, entrepreneurship, and kids—as an employee benefit—has short- and long-term rewards. For companies interested in creating innovative—and inexpensive—benefit packages, this may be one of the best bargains of the decade.

Black women represent the largest major segment of black employment, yet of all black working mothers, 53 percent live in poverty.

*Cydney Shields and Leslie Shields, *Work, Sister, Work* (New York: Simon & Schuster, 1994), p. 20.

ADD TO THE VIDEO RECORD OF WOMEN

There is still not enough video material available for teaching girls about their economic options as adults. Help enlarge the body of materials available—locally and nationally. Next time your company creates a video that includes stories about women in your company, have that part edited as a separate piece, and make it available as a "role model series." Over time your collection will be valuable to local libraries, classrooms, and girls organizations.

Or order existing videos about women business owners (contact the National Association of Women Business Owners, the National Association of Female Executives, the Business Enterprise Trust, and An Income of Her Own) and donate them to school and community libraries. "If I can't see it, I can't be it," said Sojourner Truth. Help girls SEE the options for their future.

Irma Bautista lived for a while in a shelter for battered women. Formerly the owner of a restaurant in the Philippines, she was an immigrant mother with two children, a failed marriage, and homeless. Thanks to the Homeless Women's Economic Development Project in San Francisco, Irma was able to obtain $10,000 in loans, which enabled her to purchase and renovate an existing Filipino restaurant in San Francisco's Mission District.

She had only been in business for a month when her estranged husband appeared at the restaurant and attacked her and other members of her family with a knife. Irma was hospitalized and, unable to operate her business while healing, was forced to close it.

But the other women who had gone through the Homeless Women's Project with Irma continued to provide emotional support, and the organizations that supported her with loans to open her restaurant secured additional funds. With their help and her own apparently indomitable will, Irma reopened her restaurant. Irma's Pampanga Restaurant now enjoys a strong, steady clientele, and if you are in the Bay Area you might drop by for lunch!

DISTRIBUTE NEWS ABOUT GIRLS

Make your bills more palatable to your clients: include something of value! Next time you send out bills, include information about girls: a reading list, a list of programs serving girls, a wish list for local girls organziations, information about a fundraiser for girls, or an update on your own actions on behalf of economic power for girls. Companies are important role models and this is an area that needs business leadership.

PART 4

THINGS TO DO FOR THE COUNTRY

"Think Globally, Act Locally" is the advice we get from bumper stickers—and as bumper-sticker philosophy goes, it's good advice. But improving the economic future of girls will take more than local action. Economic well-being and opportunity come from working together at the grassroots level; from massive education efforts, from policy that is girl-focused (not welfare focused), and from agreed-upon national goals that make economic empowerment for young women a commitment of the twenty-first century.

The ideas in this section are intended to help realize a vision, a vision that sees young women not on a pedestal or as mythic ideals, as in Victorian tales, and not as victims, as in more contemporary social politics, but as living, breathing, equal people with the right to dream, to be, and to grow.

Exercise your responsibility as a citizen—employ just one of the suggestions that follow to build the kind of future for young women that you would wish for a girl you know.

Lisa Conti is the visionary behind Shaman Pharmaceuticals, an alternative drug company that researches drugs drawn from the rain forest. Conti came up with the idea while working for a venture capital firm looking for bio-tech investments. Sitting in the lobby of one such firm, she was browsing through a copy of Smithsonian and happened on an article about the destruction of the rain forests.

Frustrated with the time-consuming testing methods used by most conventional pharmaceutical companies, it occurred to her that by testing plants used by shamans, she could considerably shorten the time required for standard research, improve investment opportunities, and support the work of ethno-botanists concerned about the dissolution of the rain forest ecosystem. The day after coming to this realization, she quit her job.

Conti has raised over $70 million dollars to help support Shaman Pharmaceuticals research. Several drugs are already in clinical trials, including one that treats childhood respiratory infections and another that is being tested as a treatment for herpes.

UNIT 71

JOIN NATIONAL ORGANIZATIONS THAT ADVOCATE FOR GIRLS

Get involved with a national organization concerned about the needs of girls: American Association of University Women (202-785-7700); the Ms. Foundation (212-742-2300); Girls Inc. (212-689-3700); Girl Scouts of the USA (212-852-8000); and An Income of Her Own (800-350-2978) are just a few of the organizations that do research on, advocate for, and work directly with girls. Support them with your time, write a check, learn about them and talk about them in public forums so others know what they do and why they do it.

During the holidays, add them to your giving list— make a contribution in the name of a young woman you want to support and tell her what you have done and why. Use this as an opportunity to talk about advocacy, collective action, and philanthropy as tools for both women's economic empowerment and as responsible citizen action.

In 1990 the average yearly income of a male high school dropout was a meager $8,349. But female dropouts were even more economically disadvantaged: they earned a measly $3,109.*

*Myra and David Sadker, _Failing at Fairness_ (New York: Scribner's, 1994), p. 119.

UNIT 72

Advocacy for girls on the national level is as important as on the local level. Write to the President and the First Lady, make sure they are cognizant of your concerns about the economic well-being of girls. Be sure to write to your senators and representatives and let them know you pay attention to votes that affect the economic empowerment—and disempowerment—of girls. Funding for gender equity, support for the women's division of the Small Business Administration, the health, education, and well-being of girls are all issues that congressional representatives must know cannot be traded away.

Find out the names of committee chairs who have an impact on legislation that affects young women. Write, send e-mail, fax. Your voice and your pen are urgently needed to help Congress keep girls on a high-priority list.

Jeannette Scollard has limitless energy, reserves of good humor, and a capacity for imagination that have helped her as an owner of a lamp socket factory in Hong Kong, a television station in Little Rock, Arkansas, a fishing company in the Caribbean, and restaurants in Florida and St. John. All told she has started, developed, and sold more than a dozen different businesses in the last decade.

But this seemingly tireless entrepreneur does more than start companies—she also has a strong social agenda. She was the founding director of Milestone House, a home for disadvantaged girls in California, and is on the steering committee of the SBA's mentoring program. Jeannette has written The Self-Employed Woman: How to Start Your Own Business and Gain Control of Your Life *(published by Simon & Schuster) and is developing written entrepreneurial materials—in Hindi— for the 400 million women in India.*

UNIT 73

USE YOUR VOICE!

If you sit on a board, make sure that girls are on the agenda—somewhere, sometime, somehow. If your company doesn't yet participate in Take Our Daughters to Work Day, speak up and help them get involved. As you prepare to vote in the next election, ask the candidates what they have done for girls. If you subscribe to a magazine, write and ask what their editorial plans are for covering girls. In other words, remember that you have a voice, and that it must be exercised to make a difference. And whether you are on the board of a *Fortune* 500 company or one of millions of subscribers to a national magazine, it is the cumulative effect of our voices, speaking on behalf of the next generation of women, that will give them the attention and resources they will need to grow into healthy, contributing adults.

Although a former art teacher and artist whose work has been sold in galleries and exhibited in museums around the country, Terri Lonier's entrepreneurial development began in 1981, when personal computers were first introduced to the general public. Enamored of the new technology, Terri discovered that the combination of her aesthetic sensibilities, communication skills, and her interest in computers allowed her to create bridges between art, design, technology, and individuals interested in entrepreneurial pursuits. She became a resource to entrepreneurs needing a guide to integrate these three very powerful, formerly separate, fields.

From her home in New York, Terri has become a national resource to the new—and growing—breed she calls soloists; entrepreneurs who go it alone, without the traditional structures of space, organizations, and employees. Spending more on communication than on rent, these new entrepreneurs have all the old challenges of business combined with a pack of new ones. Terri's consulting practice and her books, Working Solo and the Working Solo Sourcebook are vital tools for the entrepreneur starting out on her solo journey.

Recently, Terri became more accessible to entrepreneurs everywhere with her new on-line service, Working Solo. She demonstrates something she believes: that by pursuing "passion centers" along with "profit centers" the new entrepreneur can gain both personal fulfillment as well as economic well-being. To learn more about Terri's resources for entrepreneurs, write to Portico Press, P.O. Box 190, New Paltz, New York 12561.

UNIT 74

LOBBY FOR AN EXHIBIT ON GIRLS

Start a letter-writing campaign to the Smithsonian Museum in Washington, D.C. Ask for a traveling exhibit on the lives of girls, with a special focus on their economic lives. Suggest they begin prior to the colonial era and examine pre-history as well as contemporary issues. Urge them to make this a national priority. Create a sample letter of your proposal and make copies for five of your friends. Ask each of them to have five of their friends send letters to the museum, and five of their friends, etc. The women's communications network is powerful when tapped. Let's set a goal: how about an exhibit in 1997? If your friends won't write a letter of their own, maybe they'll sign yours. Both Judy Chicago's exhibit, "The Dinner Party," which traveled in 1977, and "I Have a Dream," the photographs of black women that was a touring exhibit in 1991, brought national attention to the lives of women. A similar effort is now needed to call attention to the economic and social lives of girls.

When a woman divorces, her income drops by 74 percent; when a man divorces, his income increases by 42 percent.*

*Jo Ann Lordahl, *Money Meditations for Women* (Berkeley, California: Celestial Arts, 1994), p. 275.

NOMINATE GIRLS

Is there a national board you know of looking for young people? Is the Rotary trying to send a young person to a national convention? Is there an opportunity to send a student to a forum of some kind? Have you nominated a young woman for a fellowship or a stint as a Senate intern?

Remember to give girls oportunities for exposure and participation on the national stage. Whether as volunteers for the White House Conference on Small Business or as student observers for such activities as a newspaper convention or your local industry's national convention, girls will absorb a great deal of information and experience that will broaden their horizons.

Yonne Tiger is a member of the Cherokee Nation, who lives in Tahlequah, Oklahoma. At the age of 16 she attended an An Income of Her Own conference on entrepreneurship for teen women and left determined to start a business of her own. With a loan from her parents and the ear—and counsel—of another woman entrepreneur, she located a building near the local community college and opened a nail care and tanning salon. A year later Yonne attended an entrepreneurial summer camp and, now understanding more about the intricacies of running a business, decided she wanted to attend college.

That fall, Yonne had to find a way to manage her business—she still owed her parents money for the start-up—and find time for school and study. By age nineteen, Yonne had experienced business dilemmas and challenges that women twice her age have yet to encounter. Her willingness to take a risk, seek her own economic future, as well as an education, makes her a true leader of the next generation.

ENVISION

Think and talk about a national vision for girls. Think so big it makes you uncomfortable. (Or, to paraphrase Oprah: Make it shine so much it will hurt your eyes!) Imagine a five- or ten- or twenty-billion dollar fund for girls. What would you do with such a resource? Imagine a national week—or a month, how about a century?—in celebration of girls. Advocate for a national network of shelters for homeless girls or girls who are victims of violence. Think about a strategy—political, social, financial, that will give girls experiences that help them be all they can be.

Vivian Shimoyama had been a marketing manager for a large consumer products company for a number of years. But as the glass ceiling became more intractable throughout the eighties, she felt an increasing need to bring her vision—a more just and equal world for all—in line with her life's work. Putting her marketing skills to work, she left the life of a corporate woman behind to create Breakthru Unlimited.

Perhaps her best known product line is the "Glass Ceiling" line of jewelry and office accessories. This "jewelry with a cause" was created to bring about awareness of the invisible barriers we all face. The artwork is worn and displayed by many prominent women and men across the United States. Vivian articulates her mission this way:

We strive for excellence,
Yet at times we may not see
    that invisible barrier to our advancement . . .
The Glass Ceiling!
It takes belief in ourselves and
    a leap of faith.
For then we make a difference and
    reach our vision of
Breakthru! . . . Beyond the Glass Ceiling!

For information about her products, call 310-545-5375.

- - - - - - - - - - - - - - -

KEEP AMERICA SHARP

Supply your elected representatives with copies of studies and articles related to the economic well-being of girls. Write letters to the editors of national magazines: *Time, Fortune, People,* etc., any time you think they have misrepresented real life for girls, overlooked girls altogether, or missed an opportunity to cover an important development related to girls. In other words, act like a press agent for girls.

Women do two-thirds of the world's work, yet they earn only one-tenth of the world's income.*

*Anne Firth Murray, "Poor But Powerful," *Foundation News*, Dec. 1988, p. 58.

PAY ATTENTION: USE YOUR POWER AS A CONSUMER

When the talking Barbie doll came out with, "Math is hard," parents and educators were up in arms immediately and it didn't take Mattel long to realize they had made a pretty serious faux pas. But girls get similar messages daily in more subtle—if no less powerful—ways. Vigilance is a responsibility to girls. Is there a television commercial that is particularly offensive? Is her school text so old that it carries all the outmoded, constricting messages about what girls can and should do? Radio deejays and TV commentators are ubiquitous—and often not especially girl-friendly. With all due respect to the First Amendment, it's important to give advertisers and the media feedback when they are using public forums to undermine the power and esteem of girls.

Kate Lytle "inherited" her racquet-stringing business from brother Jesse when he left for college. She had been involved from the very start of the business, when her parents agreed to loan Jesse $600 to buy a used Prince Stringing Machine. At the time, there was much family discussion about whether this could be a profitable business, how Jesse would find clients, and how many racquets it would take to pay back the loan. Jesse calculated that if he charged $10 per racquet (plus the cost of materials), and paid his parents $5, it would only take 120 racquets to repay the interest-free loan. Since he expected to average eight or more racquets per week, the loan could be retired within four months.

When Kate took over the business, Jesse didn't ask her to buy the stringing machine. From the first racquet, she could "retain" $10 from each sale. When the family went to Nantucket Island for the summer, they took the stringing machine with them. Kate posted notices at the tennis club and found that she could make more money with this business than in any other summer job available to a fifteen-year-old.

Nevertheless, Kate finds that there are times when she would rather baby-sit for less money than carry the responsibility of the racquet-stringing business: "The racquets feel like they're hanging over my head. My customers want them back within a few days and I feel their deadlines on top of homework deadlines." Despite the pressure, Kate isn't ready to abandon the business: "I'm more interested in making money than Jesse ever was; it's just that I want to keep it as manageable as possible during school."

RECONSIDER SUCCESS

Is the one who comes in first always the winner? Is having *more* a mark of superiority? Historically, success has been represented by fairly standard measures: a spot on the *Fortune* 500, most games won in a season, most money earned in a company. . . . Alternative values that respect the accommodation of work to meet family needs or profits that are not maximized at the expense of environment or community are examples of "success rethought." Only by reconsidering our most ingrained assumptions can we begin to change the world we have created for our daughters and integrate economic justice into our notions of economic development.

Like Stacey Kabat (described earlier), Wendy Kopp is a social entrepreneur with a vision. She is the founder of Teach America, the national organization devoted to reinvigorating the teaching profession and the education of young people. Wendy was just twenty-three years old when she started to work on her vision. Fueled by funding from both private donors and large foundations, Wendy galvanized large numbers of the so-called Generation X to enter a profession that seemed to have lost prestige and honor.

Since 1989, Teach America has placed over 2,300 young people as teachers, reaching over 500,000 students in 400 schools around the country. Kopp reports, "They aid teachers, tutor students, and serve as role models to thousands of other young people who want to make a contribution to community." For more information on Teach America, call 212-789-9289.

BONE UP ON WELFARE REFORM

Get knowledgeable about welfare reform. Slogans do not a policy make and truly effective reform depends on voters who have read, listened, and explored the many dimensions of welfare. As welfare policy affects girls and women first, we have a special responsibility to make sure old stereotypes don't affect new strategies for change. Lynn Woolsey of California was the first AFDC recipient to be elected to Congress—and informed on this issue. She reminds us there are three groups of welfare recipients: the disabled, ill, or mentally ill who cannot go to work; people who have fallen on hard times and need a safety net to get through that part of their lives; and generational welfare recipients who need a broader, deeper set of services to get off welfare.

Call the League of Women Voters for studies and recommendations they have on the subject. Or contact the Working Group on Welfare Reform, Family Support and Independence, 370 L'Enfant Plaza SW, 7th Fl., Washington, D.C. 20047. Or call Wider Opportunities for Women (202-638-3143) to receive a copy of the Act for Family Development and Independence created by the Practitioners Panel on Welfare Reform, a joint project of Wider Opportunities for Women and the Women and Poverty Project.

PART 5

THINGS GIRLS CAN DO

oday's girl is savvier, wiser, and more sophisticated than her mother was. By adolescence—and sometimes earlier—many girls face issues of life and death (guns and AIDS), health (drugs and pregnancy), and the management of hormones and heart (boyfriends, girlfriends, and family—or the lack thereof).

One way to make sure we don't raise another generation of girls whose primary hope for economic well-being is rescue by a funny-looking frog or feet that fit glass slippers, is to give them the respect they deserve and acknowledge their ability and desire to do things for themselves. The ideas in this section are intended for girls to try themselves. Young women are resourceful, full of dreams, and hungry for experiences that give them a sense of their own power and competence. Let a young woman you know browse this section and choose at will, in her own time, ways to empower herself.

On average, employed women work about two hours more per day than men do. *

*"Women in the World," *Women Organizing: A Report from the Global Fund for Women* (Palo Alto, California, 1993), p. 3.

UNIT 81

PUT YOUR BUSINESS DREAM ON PAPER

A business plan is just a way of describing on paper how you plan to make money with a dream. Do you love to write? Describe how you might produce and sell a book or a play. Are you pretty good on the computer? Describe how you can make money by working with technophobic adults in the neighborhood and making them comfortable with a computer.

Call 800-350-2978 and request an application for the National Business Plan Competition for Teens. The application provides an outline and a guide for creating a business plan that makes the exercise no more difficult than solving a good mystery or unraveling an especially intriguing puzzle.

If you need a coach, ask a high school business teacher for suggestions of adults who might make good coaches. Or forget the coach and do it on your own—you may know more than you think you do!

Gloria Steinem says of Emily Card, "She's to money what Julia Child is to cooking." A lawyer by training, Ms. Card has built her practice into a successful financial consulting business. Emily was involved in drafting the Equal Credit Opportunity Act of 1974. This contribution changed forever women's ability to obtain credit and has irrevocably altered the relationship between women and money. More than just an activist, Emily Card is an entrepreneur who really makes a difference.

A Ms. *magazine columnist from 1983 to 1989, she is also the author of* The Ms. Money Book *and co-author of the best-selling* Consumer Reports Money Book. *Emily teaches women all over the country strategies for reducing their economic vulnerability and advises them on starting and running their businesses.*

WHAT ARE YOU WORTH?

Your parents might call you priceless, your friends refer to you as a treasure, and at least one teacher would call you a "diamond in the rough." But what are you worth, in real numbers? Figure out your net worth—today. And think about what you would like it to be and how you will get there. To figure out your net worth, write down everything you own. It may be precious little right now! But did your grandmother leave you her wedding ring? Have you bought a car that you paid for? Do you have a savings account? Give everything a dollar amount and add it up.

Now figure out what you owe. Do you still have payments left on a car? Are you paying your mom back for a school loan? Do you have a dress on lay-away somewhere that you are slowly paying off? Add that all up, too.

Now subtract that last number from the first (all you are worth) and what you are left with is your *net worth*. (If it's a negative number we'd say you're in deficit or have a negative net worth.) No big deal. You have time to increase your net worth. But get on it, girl, time's awastin'! Being aware of and creating net worth is one way of taking care of yourself and letting the world know you're a sister in charge!

Audrey Rice Oliver started her first company in 1971. The Boot Broker catered to men (she thought their shoe-buying habits were more regular, if less exciting, than women's). The company was located in a prestigious shopping gallery in Denver, Colorado. She was the first African American to lease space there. But breaking new ground has become old hat for Oliver. By 1984 she had shifted into a new industry, establishing a communications firm specializing in minority and women's business program development. This prompted her to author the first Minority and Women's Business Enterprise plan approved by the U.S. Department of Transportation.

Out of that effort evolved Integrated Business Solutions, now a multimillion-dollar company providing information solutions to corporations and government. In 1992 Audrey was invited to the Little Rock Economic Conference by President Clinton. In 1993 the San Francisco Chapter of the National Association of Women Business Owners recognized her as Entrepreneur of the Year. Audrey's experiences—from retail to government service to a leader of a high-tech company—have equipped her to play on a very large stage in the world of business. But she never forgets her roots—or the needs of others. Her involvement with young women—offering guidance, inviting them to visit her company, providing support—serves as a challenge to business leaders everywhere to remember to "take time for the next generation."

UNIT 83

SAVE

Whether calories, time, trees, or dollars, life is full of saving. It may not be as much fun as a night of dancing, but there usually is a reward, which is, after all, some compensation. Set yourself a goal for saving money (even $5 a month will do for a start) and stick to it. Put the money in an account and treat it like a rabid dog— stay away from it! Let it grow. When you get to your goal, resist cashing it all in (so maybe a hot fudge sundae for reward wouldn't do too much harm) and set another goal (a biking trip cross-country perhaps? a fancier computer? a contribution to your favorite cause?).

The important thing is to get into a habit of saving that you take seriously. This is your *life* we're talking about, and unless you really do intend to marry a prince (how boring) or are the only living relative of a very rich aunt, you better start to make an economic safety net for yourself that will see you through all life's little surprises—and tell the world you know you're a woman of value!

One quarter of all widows have gone through their insurance benefits within two months; yet they live, on average, another 18.5 years.*

---

*Jo Ann Lordahl, *Money Meditations for Women* (Berkeley, California: Celestial Arts, 1994), p. 235.

UNIT 84

PRACTICE SOCIAL ENTREPRENEURSHIP

Do you volunteer on a teen hotline? Do you work once a week at an AIDS hospice? Do you serve meals at a homeless shelter? In addition to giving time, why not think of ways to give money, too? Organize a few friends to run a mighty garage sale that will benefit the organization of your choosing. (Once you get this down, you might try running one to benefit your own bottom line!)

There are a few good guidebooks on how to run a profitable garage sale—one we like is *Honey, We Need to Have a Garage Sale*, by Georgeann Manville, which can be ordered by phoning 805-646-2978. (Or tune into AIOHO on E-World for tips on running a profitable garage sale.) The main thing to know is that if you can get your homework done on time and can add, subtract, make signs, and talk to strangers (or have someone else on your team who can do some of these things) you can run a garage sale and make a real difference to the cause you support.

In October 1994, Jeanne Englehart broke ground on a new 16,500-square-foot, $1.5 million building in Grand Rapids, Michigan, that is designed to house eleven conventional classrooms and a twelfth high-tech classroom equipped with teleconferencing and satellite broadcast capabilities. Englehart is the founder of Englehart Training Centers. Her company, started in 1985, provides computer training for over 11,000 corporate employees every year, and they keep coming back for more. In 1993, she joined Productivity Point, a national consortium of independent training companies. This new affiliation has allowed her to leverage and expand her company swiftly—which explains, in part, the new building!

Like so many other women entrepreneurs, Jeanne integrates her personal values with the way she conducts her business life. Author/teacher/CEO and the 1993 winner of the Inc. 500 Entrepreneur of the Year award, Jeanne has become a national figure and a frequent speaker. Her personal favorite presentation is called From June Cleaver to Murphy Brown. . . . It traces the evolution of women's development and what that has meant to her own development as an economic being at ease in so many roles.

ADOPT A COACH

You may have a soccer coach or a drama coach, but do you have a money coach? Probably not. Why, it even sounds awful—imagine having a coach to talk to you about money! But the fact is that sometimes money is too hard to talk about at home. Another way to get an early education about your financial future is to adopt an adult who will help you think through money issues that come up, introduce you to resources that will help get you through school and someday into a house of your own, and explain words and concepts that may sound like so much boring Wall Street drivel. To find your coach, identify three adults you admire (maybe an aunt, a teacher, a friend's parent). Tell them each what you would like and ask if you can interview them (and, of course, let them interview you). Here are a few questions to get you started:

Do you handle your own finances?

Would you be willing to help me learn about money, savings, and ways to develop a good financial base?

What do you wish you had known at my age?

Do you feel confident about your ability to handle money and advise others?

You may need to remind your coach that you aren't looking for an investment counselor (if you are, you don't need this book!), but just need someone you can go to to ask questions and figure out where to get answers.

Katie Williams, a pioneer in a new industry, started with $2,000 and a handful of credit cards. Now the owner of Williams Televison Time, she bills over $60 million annually and is acknowledged as the leader in direct response television advertising—sometimes know as the infomercial business. Nordic Track, Philips Electronics, Hoover, and Mars are among her growing list of clients. "With this medium," she says, "you can't kid yourself; either it's selling or it's not and you know what's happening in a few hours."

Perhaps it is the fearlessness that one feels in her presence. Or maybe it's the accumulation of experiences collected since she was a little girl that helps her project an air of calm competence. Although she didn't receive proper credit at the time, Katie was the first "paper girl" in her hometown of Plattsburgh, New York. Since then she's had a rich and varied set of experiences—she learned transcendental meditation in Switzerland, ran a bakery in Iowa, got her degree from Cornell, and worked as a loan officer in a mortgage company.

So maybe it was no surprise that she was open to a serendipitous offer from a man just getting started in the fledgling cable industry. Buying television time for him to teach people how to buy real estate, Katie Williams was soon an expert in the new world of infomercials. Now she's shooting for $100 million in billings. "Maintaining relationships is central to this business," she says. "Much work is still done on a handshake. It's an old-fashioned way of doing a brand-new business that I like." Old fashioned perhaps, but she's got more than just a foot in the future—she is the future!

UNIT 86

STATE YOUR WORTH

The local grocery store offers to pay you $6 an hour if you take a job there. You can be a lifeguard next summer and get a great tan and minimum wage. If you waitress you'll make whatever tips the clientele leaves behind, plus a base wage from the restaurant. But what if someone asks you to do a project for them and says, "What do you want to be paid?" *What will you say?*

Girls and women almost always undervalue themselves, so before you get in that position, practice in your head and with your friends. Let's say you make the best chocolate torte in America and you've been asked to make ten of them for a private party. Or you've been asked to house-sit for your best friend's mother while the family is on vacation.

First, find out what other companies or people might charge for the same service. Figure out what it will cost you to do whatever has been asked (how much does flour cost; will you need to take the bus to your friend's house?). Then decide what dollar amount feels right and is competitive—that is, not unfairly different from what other people would charge. Then give that figure in a strong voice and don't change unless there is a good reason to do so (such as your friend's mother offers to take you to Hawaii with them over school break if you work for nothing now!)

Nationally, 68 percent of male faculty members enjoy tenure, while only 45 percent of women enjoy this lifetime job security.*

*Myra and David Sadker, *Failing at Fairness* (New York: Scribner's, 1994), p. 166.

CREATE A PORTFOLIO

Eventually someone will suggest that you do a resumé. It's a good idea. Do it. But also think about compiling a portfolio. Much as artists put together pieces of their best work for potential buyers to view, you can put together samples of your work that will give a potential employer (or client) a sense of your range of talents.

Did you organize the class fashion show? Put in a copy of the program and any press reports describing it. Are you a reporter with a teen paper? Add samples of your writing. Create a summary describing the kinds of skills you have: are you computer literate, do you sketch or draw? Think of all you have done that shows you can organize, think, manage, create, or complete a task, the generic underpinning of all work.

Ranny Riley started her career as a research psychologist with the Stanford Research Institute. With two different companies to her credit, she has embarked on a third that she hopes will make the next stage of life for baby-boomer women more enjoyable. LifeLines was established to develop and market COMPASS, an interactive kit for women in perimenopause and menopause. Recognizing that baby boomers are entering menopause and demanding better choices for their health care, she created a product that borrows from five different health approaches.

A baby boomer herself, Ranny is attuned to the needs of her generation, and has embarked on a mission to help all women journeying through the middle years to enjoy their lives with the same gusto that marked earlier life stages. For more inormation about the LifeLines Institute call 415-929-8150.

PICTURE YOURSELF IN BUSINESS

Imagine the following scenario:

"I am sitting behind a desk made just for me. The chair feels exactly right and everything on the desk is in easy reach. . . . I turn on my computer to review the agenda for the day. I see that later I will meet with a banker to discuss a business loan. Later, my partner and I will consider new ways to improve our company's recycling program. . . . The product I have invented will make in-town travel easier for people who are physically challenged. The head of the sales team wants to report on the status of a sales contract, which if approved, will enable my company to hire and employ another two hundred people. . . . Tonight I am being honored by the local Chamber of Commerce for our student intern program. I feel powerful and influential. I make a lot of money and I am very much involved in giving back to the community. I have fun and know that my family is proud of me and supportive of my accomplishments."

Sit with these images for a few minutes. How do you feel? Have you thought about yourself as a company owner before?

Author-educator Judy Galbraith founded Free Spirit Publishing in 1983 to provide resources for young people in the areas of education, mental health, and social responsibility. More than a decade later, Free Spirit, located in Minneapolis, Minnesota, has become the leader in "Self-Help for Kids." Formerly a teacher of gifted children and teens, Judy had a vision to use the vehicle of publishing to help kids help themselves.

Among the subjects covered by the books and publications from Free Spirit: stress management for teens, assertiveness for children, and getting along at home and school. In concert with her concern for kids, Free Spirit has donated more than 1,000 books to New York Cares, an organization that distributes books, free of charge, to nonprofit organizations that help children and families in distress.

UNIT 89

START A WOMEN'S FINANCE CLUB AT SCHOOL

Invite a few of your friends to start a support group to talk about money and your future. Maybe you'll decide to learn more about investments or start some money-making projects together. Or you could learn more about cooperative models of business and what women in third world countries have done with microenterprise to support themselves. Or maybe you'll just share your feelings and fears about managing money. The main thing is to find a way to start learning about your economic future in a way that is comfortable and fun.

Although 75 percent of women work outside the home, 80 percent are still clustered in 20 percent of the 410 job categories classified by the U.S. Department of Labor.*

*Molly Mead, *Worlds Apart* (Women in Philanthropy and the Boston Women's Fund, 1994), p. 4.

TRACK YOUR ATTITUDE

You think business is boring? Money irrelevant? You recoil at the thought of keeping track of what you spend every week? You're a financephobe! Get over it! Track your journey from financephobe to finance*phile* by keeping a journal in which you talk about your feelings and reactions to anything that has to do with money.

Try to understand where those feelings come from and what you need to be more confident when the subject of money and economic well-being comes up.

Talk with friends and see if they share any of your feelings. After six months, reread your original material and see if your feelings have changed at all. Brainstorm ways to develop more knowledge about business and the financial side of career planning.

800-SHY-PROD. That's the number any teen can dial to buy products related to hygiene and menstruation. As an adolescent girl, the most dreaded part of Katrina Cabral's life was the monthly visit to the grocery store to buy sanitary napkins. The trip to the checkout counter was almost unbearable to this shy young woman. Most of the time her mother picked up the necessary items and spared her the pain of the task. Then her mother became ill and was in the hospital for a protracted stay.

Katrina's dad tried to help out. "Is there anything you need, dear?" he'd ask before going to the store. No, she'd reply, wishing with all her might that she could just call a number and have the things delivered to her door.

In 1992, at the age of twenty-five, she decided that other adolescents probably still felt the way she had. So she started Shy Produx, a service for girls that allows them to order products sent to them in a plain wrapper—complete with a free surprise gift packaged inside. That's to satisfy nosy brothers who want to know what came in the mail!

DEVELOP YOUR HERSTORY

Learn more about some of the women mentioned in this book: Margot Fraser, the woman who introduced Birkenstocks to America; Madame C. J. Walker, first self-made African-American woman millionaire in this country; Ruth Owades, founder of two companies—Gardener's Eden and Calyx and Corolla; Leann Chinn, founder of a chain of restaurants in Minneapolis; Laura Sanchez, owner of El Rey Foods.

See what they have in common, what makes each of them unique, and what about their business is interesting to you.

Chloe Breyer, Lesley Crutchfield, and Heather McLeod are the three twentysomething co-founders of Who Cares, *"A Journal of Service and Action." With a grant from the Echoing Green Foundation and the support of the photographer Annie Leibowitz and Harvard professor Robert Coles, the three young women made their own, post-Harvard graduation jobs.* Who Cares *covers the community service and social responsibility movement. Their readers are, they say, "Partners in change, the magazine for people who do."*

Who Cares is not the founding team's first venture. Their first magazine was There and Back, *by and for students who have studied abroad (McLeod spent a year in France on a Rotary scholarship; Crutchfield did volunteer work in Cambia; and Breyer taught English at a Tibetan monastery.) And it was through that first experience in publishing that each of them began to learn about the power of giving back.*

Their goal for Who Cares *is "to get it into the hands of every young activist." The magazine was named one of ten best new titles for the 1994 Alternative Press awards. Call 202-628-1691 for subscription information.*

PASS IT ON

Whatever you learn about economic power, managing money, entrepreneurship, or business, pass it on to a girl who is younger than you. Ella Williams, founder of Ms. Ella's World Class Cheesecake (and the founder of Aegir Systems, an engineering company in southern California) started Ms. Ella's with the goal of being able to educate one hundred minority students. She always tells young people in her audience, "Find just one child younger than you and make sure you give back what was given to you."

In 1983 the typical female lawyer earned 89 percent of a male lawyer's income; by 1991, that figure had fallen to 75 percent.*

*Myra and David Sadker, *Failing at Fairness* (New York: Scribner's, 1994), p. 166.

UNIT 93

GET CRITICAL!

The companies that you buy products from are very knowledgeable about you. They've been following you since you were a very little girl. And they know, for example, that teen women (ages 13–19) spend an average of $2,938 per year on clothing and jewelry, food and snacks, records, tapes, books, hobbies, entertainment, and cosmetics.

What you may not know is that this means you have a lot of financial clout. Imagine if you and all your friends decided you were not going to buy a particular brand of jeans because the company didn't give its female employees a safe working environment, or think about what would happen if you all decided that a particular record company had just too many songs that trash women and you wouldn't buy their label until they cleaned up their act. THAT'S POWER!

Before you respond to the next cool ad on TV or the display at the mall that tempts you to spend the money you had meant to add to your savings account, remember that the company probably spent a lot of money to get you to make a decision that's in THEIR best interest—is it in your best interest?

B. LaRae Orullian was the first national president of the Girl Scouts of the USA to be employed outside the home. As the CEO of the Women's Bank in Denver, Colorado, and CEO of Equitable Bankshares in Colorado, she represented a decidedly new point of view among Girl Scouts. "You need more than the campfire and singing and sitting around the fire," she was quoted as saying. "Our troops are heavily into math and science projects."

Though LaRae finished her term as national president in 1994, she was an important role model for millions of young women. And in 1992 she was selected as Entrepreneur of the Year by Entrepreneurs of America, Inc., and Inc. magazine.

UNIT 94

BE YOURSELF

In the end, our greatest power emerges when we know who we are, pay attention to our inner voices, say what we think, and own our opinions, however unusual or misunderstood. Some of the world's most successful people have been laughed at, disliked, or ignored because their ideas were unfamiliar, strange, or unexpected.

Ruth Owades's boss told her that her idea for a mail-order catalog for the home gardener would never work. Millions of dollars in sales later, after she'd left him in the dust, she proved him wrong. We would add that if people aren't laughing at you, you aren't saying anything very unusual. So let your voice be loud and strong, dare to try things that may fail, and make sure you follow YOUR path, not the path that someone else sets for you.

Josée Covington of Richmond, Virginia, is a native of Luxembourg. That's the reason, she explains, her travel business has grown over twenty-seven years to employ seventy-five people, "Luxembourg is a grand duchy that is only one thousand square miles in size. From the day you are born, you are a traveler—a half-hour south by car, you are in France; a half-hour east, you are in Germany; and a half-hour west, you are in Belgium!"

As a young woman Josée worked in New York for American Express. "I learned both the mechanics of planning trips and the theory of travel there—and I knew Europe like the back of my hand." This combination of knowledge and experience landed her a job in another travel agency when she moved to Richmond, where her husband was in dental school. But finding herself blocked and thwarted at every turn, she decided to open her own company. With money borrowed from her grandmother back in Luxembourg, Josée started Covington International Travel in 1967. Hers was one of the first companies to computerize in the seventies. Over the last two decades she has expanded her company several times to meet demand and the changing nature of travel among her clients. A wife and mother, Josée employs two sons in her business, and her third son, a Washington, D.C., attorney, sits on her board of directors. "If there is a downside of owning a business," she says, "I haven't found it."

UNIT 95

FIND THE HIDDEN VALUE IN YOUR HOBBIES

Do you collect coins? Do you love gardening? Are you a neatnik? Do classmates call you for homework help? Are you handy with bike repairs?

While it's important not to commercialize all the things you love, it's equally important not to overlook the earning potential of your passions. Making money while you pursue your dreams is not a bad strategy.

Take inventory of the things you like to do, then explore how what you do has an interest and a value to other people. If you collect coins, maybe you can be a finder for other collectors. Or maybe you write a newsletter for other teen collectors, which advertisers pay for who want to reach your teen colleagues.

If you love gardening, maybe you can supply local restaurants with a specialty green or miniature vegetables. Before you start to look for a job, take stock of what you love. There may be a job hidden inside a hobby!

In 1995 the National Foundation for Women Business Owners reported that 38 percent of the women business owners they surveyed stated, "the most significant challenge facing women business owners is being taken seriously."

The number one priority of teen women surveyed in AIOHO programs? Being taken seriously.

DEVELOP ASSETS

And we don't mean a better figure. Ownership, whether of savings deposits, your mother's heirloom jewelry, a piece of land, a business, or a book that pays royalties, is one of the smartest ways for girls to start building an economic safety net. Think you're too young?

Go talk to that finance coach we discussed earlier. Perhaps cooperative ownership is right for you. There are many models and methods of creating value and establishing a financial cushion. But many girls put off ownership, waiting either until "they're older" or waiting to buy something with a mate. Neither strategy recognizes the reality of lives filled with unexpected turns and bumps. Build assets. Readiness and a mate will follow!

Chrissie Correia did a number of things as favors for friends and family: she made dolls with beautiful, detailed costumes and she did translations for recent immigrants whose first language was Portuguese or Creole who needed help at the grocery store or the doctor's office. But after going through a program offered by the National Foundation for Teaching Entrepreneurship, she decided to turn those activities into a business. When asked about the shift in emphasis, she explained, "I wanted to be taken seriously. I'm confined to a wheelchair and people looked at me and put me down as handicapped. But I believed in myself and decided to make a business out of my hobbies to prove I could amount to something."

There's little doubt that Chrissie will "amount to something." This Brockton, Massachusetts, teenager speaks English, Portuguese, and Creole. She has more clients than time and priorities that will serve her well. When interviewed by students on a school broadcast called "Picture Yourself in Business," Chrissie made it clear that, for now, school comes first. But on graduating from high school she intends to develop her businesses and direct the entire operation by herself. Now she works after school and on her vacations. And in between all her other responsibilities she also counsels other teens with disabilities. Her advice? Never let anyone tell you you can't do something!"

ESTABLISH GOOD CREDIT

The age of information has made it virtually impossible to hide from bad habits. If you make a promise to pay something—and don't—it's a promise that that broken promise will haunt you. Establishing good credit will open doors for you that could otherwise remain closed. A seventeen-year-old graduate of Camp $tart-Up, AIOHO's summer entrepreneurship camp, planned to lease a "Bobcat," a piece of construction equipment that could be rented in turn to homeowners who wanted to do their own home yard building.

Asked how she was going to make such a significant purchase, the camper replied, "I have already gotten a car loan from a bank in my town and paid it back. They know they can count on me."

Such confidence and awareness in a seventeen-year-old is pretty remarkable. But that kind of confidence comes from a good credit history.

Linda Ellerbee, Madonna, Whoopie, Oprah, Fran Drescher
. . . Most people think of these women as celebrities, but
they are also smart and effective entrepreneurs. Fran
Drescher (a.k.a. The Nanny) owns a successful bread bak-
ery and distribution company in Santa Monica, California;
Madonna owns Maverick Productions and runs her own
shows—literally. Oprah's Harpo Productions makes her
perhaps the wealthiest woman business owner in the coun-
try. And Linda Ellerbee of Lucky Duck Productions started
out in the floor basement of her house with her partner,
Rolfe Tessen, an office manager, and with only their sav-
ings for capital. She did Maxwell House Coffee commer-
cials for a while to keep the company afloat. While not
everyone approved, she was pragmatic about what she had
to do to keep the company going. Today she employs more
than twenty people and has moved from the basement to a
modern office building from which she produces "Real
News for Kids" on Nickelodeon.

Ellerbee and her entertainment industry colleagues have
much to teach about what goes on behind the glitz. Like
highly paid basketball players who know their seasons may
be few, these women have had the wisdom to create busi-
nesses that will support them for the long term.

ACT UP

Being nice is important. Working cooperatively with others is critical. But sometimes, the person who acts up, or announces "the empress has no clothes," or in some other way rocks the boat, is the one who exhibits real leadership.

Gloria Steinem, Wilma Mankiller, Hillary Clinton, Angela Davis, Roseanne, and Whoopie Goldberg are just a tiny sample of the women of our time who have "acted up" and made a difference in the bargain. Knowing when and how to act up to get the most impact for your trouble is an instinct that comes from time and experience. But the only way to learn how to stay in a rocking boat is to practice.

*Dropping out of school gives a girl a 90 percent chance of living in poverty as an adult.**

*Molly Mead, *Worlds Apart* (Women in Philanthropy and the Boston Women's Fund, 1994), p. 4.

LEARN A NEW LANGUAGE

If you are taking Spanish or French or Japanese, you know what it means to learn a new language. To give yourself some power, learn another language—this one is called business. Income? Net profit? Stockholders? Market survey?

Just words to describe things you already know. *Income* is the money you make when you sell those pots you threw on the wheel. *Net profit* is what's left over when you've paid for the clay and everything else that went into making the pot (including your time). And a *market survey* is just a way of describing what an advertising exec does when interviewing you and your friends about which style of jeans you prefer.

Like learning French so you can tool around Paris someday, learning business will let you tool around the world of money and finance. Call 800-350-2978 for a "Guide to Business Language for Teen Women."

AFTERWORD

For those wishing to help prepare girls for a future filled with many more options and quality-of-life decisions—this is the guide. If each person who reads this book implements just two or three of the 99 ideas, then never again, at least in the United States, will women and girls' career choices be limited by anything other than their own dreams.

This book also puts to rest any possible excuse by those who want to help but did not know where to begin. The options in this book are as simple as having a conversation or watching a movie—with a purpose!

I encourage you either to begin or to continue the momentum of positive actions toward giving girls more professional, humanistic role models. If you have ever wondered if one person can make a difference, you can believe it now.

Patty DeDominic, CEO, PDQ Personnel Services, Inc.;
President, National Association of Women
Business Owners 1994–1995

RESOURCES FOR GIRLS' ECONOMIC EMPOWERMENT

Use this section as a quick reference guide to the programs, people, and materials that support our dreams for the future of girls.

ABOUT AN INCOME OF HER OWN

An Income of Her Own is a national organization that offers entrepreneurship education and economic literacy to girls and young women. Starting with the proposition that "business isn't spinach" (that is, business is not just about bottom lines and profit but also adventure, creation, and the realization of one's dreams for self and community), AIOHO programs are designed to be fun and informative.

Formed in 1992, in the aftermath of the American Association of University Women study (How Schools Shortchange Girls, 1991), and with a growing awareness of the economic vulnerability of teen women, the organization's aim is to build awareness and the skills for economic responsibility and entrepreneurship among teen women.

Today, AIOHO offers awareness-building conferences, school programs, summer camps (Camp $tart-Up), satellite broadcasts, on-line service, a National Business Plan Competition, as well as games, videos, and other materials that parents, youth leaders, and other adults concerned about the well-being of girls may use with ease and enjoyment.

AIOHO has attracted attention nationwide with articles in the *Washington Post, L.A. Times, Black Enterprise, Hispanic*

Business, Inc. magazine, and other national publications, in addition to television spots on CNN, Working Woman Television, and National Public Radio's Marketplace. For more information about the organization and how to become involved, call 800-350-2978 or write to AIOHO, P.O. Box 987, Santa Barbara, CA 93102.

BOOKS AND ARTICLES

Astin, Helen S., and Carole Leland. *Women of Influence; Women of Vision* (San Francisco: Jossey-Bass, 1991).

Bernstein, Daryl. *Better Than a Lemonade Stand* (Hillsboro, OR: Beyond Words Publishing, 1992).

Bettina, Flores. *Chiquita's Cocoon: A Cinderella Complex for the Latina Woman* (Pepper Vine Press, 1990).

Bingham, Mindy, and Sandy Stryker. *Things Will Be Different For My Daughter* (New York: Penguin Books, 1995).

Bundles, A'lelia. *Madame C. J. Walker* (New York: Chelsea Press, 1991).

Card, Emily. *The Ms. Money Book* (New York: Dutton, 1990).

Downie, Diane, Twila Slesnick, and Jean Kerr Stenmark. *Math for Girls and Other Problem Solvers* (Berkeley, CA: Lawrence Hall of Science, 1981).

Girls Incorporated. *Spinnerets and Know-How, Operation SMART Planning Guide* (New York: Girls Incorporated, 1990).

Hawken, Paul. *Growing a Business* (New York: Simon & Schuster, 1987).

Hawken, Paul. *The Ecology of Commerce* (New York: HarperBusiness, 1994).

Helgeson, Sally. *The Female Advantage: Women's Ways of Leadership* (New York: Doubleday Currency, 1990).

Kurtzig, Sandra. *CEO* (New York: W. W. Norton, 1991).

Lonier, Terri. *Working Solo* and *The Working Solo Sourcebook* (New Paltz, NY: Portico Press, 1994).

Lordahl, Jo Ann. *Money Meditations for Women* (Berkeley, CA: Celestial Arts, 1994).

Malkind, Samuel. *Commodities for Kids of All Ages* (New York: Vantage Press, 1993).

Mann, Judy. *The Difference* (New York: Warner Books, 1994).

Menzies, Linda, Oren Jenkins, and Rickell Fisher. *A Teen's Guide to Business* (New York: MasterMedia, 1992).

Nichols, Nancy, ed. *Reach for the Top: Women and the Changing Facts of Work Life* (Cambridge: Harvard University Press, 1994).

Peters, Tom. *The Tom Peters Seminar and Getting to WOW!* (New York: Vintage, 1994).

Roddick, Anita. *Body and Soul* (New York: Crown Publishing, 1991).

Rodgers, Fran S., and Charles Rodgers. "Business and the Facts of Family Life," *Harvard Business Review*, November–December 1989, pp. 121–129. Reprint No. 89610.

Rosener, Judy. "Ways Women Lead," *Harvard Business Review*, November–December 1990, pp. 119–125.

Rosener, Judy, and Marilyn Lodener. *Workforce America* (New York: Dow Jones Publishing, 1991).

Sadker, Myra, David Sadker. *Failing at Fairness: How America's Schools Cheat Girls* (New York: Scribner's, 1994).

Scott, Mary, and Howard Rothman. *Companies with a Conscience* (Birch Lane Press, 1992).

Shields, Cydney, and Leslie Shields. *Work, Sister, Work* (New York: Simon & Schuster, 1994).

ORGANIZATIONS

Academic Innovations
3463 State St., 219 T
Santa Barbara, CA 93102
805-967-0815 (ext. 892)

**American Association of
University Women**
1111 Sixteenth St., NW
Washington, D.C. 20036
800-326-2289

**American Woman's
Economic Development
Corpororation (AWED)**
1301 East Ocean Blvd. #1010
Long Beach, CA 90802
310-983-3747
AWED/Washington, D.C.
1250 24th St., #120
Washington, D.C. 20037
202-857-0091

An Income of Her Own
P.O. Box 947
Santa Barbara, CA 93102
800-350-2978

**Association of Black
Women Entrepreneurs**
1301 Kenter Ave.
Los Angeles, CA 90049
310-472-4927

**The Center for Teen
Entrepreneurs**
P.O. Box 3967
New York, NY 10163-8336
800-438-8336

EDGE
474 West 238 St., #4B
Riverdale, NY 10463

**The Entrepreneurial
Development Institute**
2025 I St. N.W., #905
Washington, D.C. 20006

Girl Scouts of the USA
420 Fifth Ave.
New York, NY 10018-2202
212-852-8000

Girls Inc.
NATIONAL HEADQUARTERS:
30 East 33rd St.
New York, NY 10016-5394
212-689-3700
email: hn3578@handsnet.org

NATIONAL RESOURCE CENTER:
441 W. Michigan St.
Indianapolis, IN 46202
317-634-7546
email: hn3580@handsnet.org
For the affiliate nearest you call
317-634-7546.

Junior Achievement, Inc.
One Education Way
Colorado Springs, CO 80906
719-540-8000

Ms. Foundation for Women
1 Wall Street
New York, NY 10005
212-742-2300
(sponsors of Take Our Daughters to
Work Day)

The National Association for Female Executives (NAFE)
30 Irving Place
New York, NY 10003
212-477-2200
(Sponsors Esteem Teams for Girls)

The National Center for American Indian Enterprises
953 East Juanita Ave.
Mesa, AZ 85204
800-423-0452

National Foundation for Women Business Owners
1377 K St. NW, #637
Washington, D.C. 20005
301-495-4975

New Moon
P.O. Box 3587
Duluth, MN 55803
218-728-5507

Third Wave
185 Franklin St.
New York, NY 10013
212-925-3400

Teen Voices
P.O. Box 6009, JFK
Boston, MA 02114

BUSINESS IDEAS

You want to help her think of an alternative to waitressing. Here are some ideas to offer:

Baby-sit babies, house plants, birds, cats, dogs, etc.
Be a clown at kid parties
Chauffeur senior citizens or people without driver's licenses
Clean houses, swimming pools, windows, cars, etc.
Clip articles for a clipping service
Deliver: newspapers, flowers, food, etc.
Design and sell T-shirts
DJ at parties and dances
Do street music, juggling, or other entertainment

Give sailing lessons, aerobics, etc.
Repair bikes
Run errands
Run garage sales
Strip furniture
Stuff envelopes for local businesses
Taxi pets to appointments
Type papers for classmates
Walk dogs
Weed gardens, mow lawns, shovel snow

VOCABULARY

The following words and phrases are intended as a beginner's business vocabulary. Make up flash cards, look up the meanings with her, or create a word game to give practice in using the words in context. Hint: *The Ms. Money Book* by Emily Card and *The Woman's Guide to Starting a Business* by Claudia Jessup and Genie Chipps are excellent sources for discovering the meanings of the words on this list.

accounts payable
accounts receivable
asset
balance sheet
break even
budget
capital
cash flow statement
client
collaboration
consumables
copyright
customer profile
debt
demographics
direct mail
distribution
entrepreneur
fixed costs
for profit business
green tax
incentive
inventory
investor
invoice
liability
market
marketing
mentor

NAWBO
net gain
net loss
nonprofit business
overhead
partnership
patent
press release
production
profit
profit margin
purchase order
quality control
receipt
regulation
renewable resources
retail
sales
SBA
social entrepreneur
social responsibility
soloist
subcontractor
sustainable resources
target market
tax
telecommuter
variable costs
wholesale

Send Us Your *No More Frogs to Kiss* Action or Story about a Woman Entrepreneur

An Income of Her Own has been nurtured and grown by women and men who care deeply about the future of the next generation of young women. They have given time, ideas, money, and heart to help build an organization whose sole mission is the economic empowerment of girls and young women. The power of grassroots organizations to give birth to and sustain a dream is one of the great miracles of community. If you would like to be part of making this dream come true, tear out this page and send it to: AIOHO, P.O. Box 987, Santa Barbara, CA 93102.

I want to help give economic power to girls. Here's my idea for action:

Tell me more about AIOHO.

Name:

Street:

City: State: Zip:

Tel.:

Fax:

On-line address:

ORDER FORM

Name:

Street:

City:

State:

Zip:

I would like to order:

___ Copies *No More Frogs to Kiss* @ $12   ($2 S&H)   ———

___ Copies An Income of Her Own Board Game @ $40   ($3 S&H)   ———

___ Information about AIOHO   No Charge

                              Local Tax   ———

                              Total   ———

Send orders to:

An Income of Her Own

P.O. Box 987

Santa Barbara, CA 93102